STARTER GUIDES

LANDSCAPE
Painting

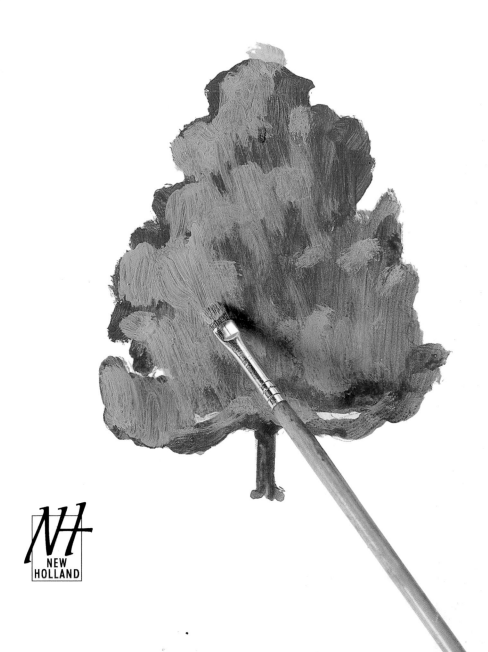

NH
NEW
HOLLAND

First published in the UK in 2006 by
New Holland Publishers (UK) Ltd
London • Cape Town • Sydney • Auckland
www.newhollandpublishers.com

Garfield House, 86–88 Edgware Road, London W2 2EA

80 McKenzie Street, Cape Town 8001, South Africa

Level 1, Unit 4, 14 Aquatic Drive, Frenchs Forest, NSW 2086, Australia

218 Lake Road, Northcote, Auckland, New Zealand

Copyright © 2006 in this edition New Holland Publishers (UK) Ltd
Original title of the book in Spanish:
Guías Para Principiantes: Pintura de Paisaje
© 2005 Parramon Ediciones, S.A.—World Rights
Published by Parramon Ediciones, S.A., Barcelona, Spain.

ISBN 1 84537 514 9

10 9 8 7 6 5 4 3 2 1

Author: Parramon's Editorial Team
Text: Gabriel Martín Roig
Photographers: Nos & Soto
Artists: Mercedes Gaspar, Gabriel Martín, Esther Olivé de Puig, Óscar
Sanchís, Carlant

Copyright 2006 of English translation by Barron's Educational Series, Inc.
English translation by Eric A. Bye, M.A.

Printed in Spain

CONTENTS

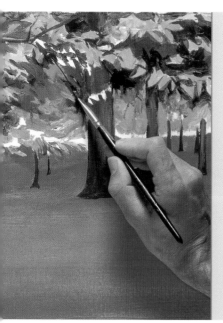

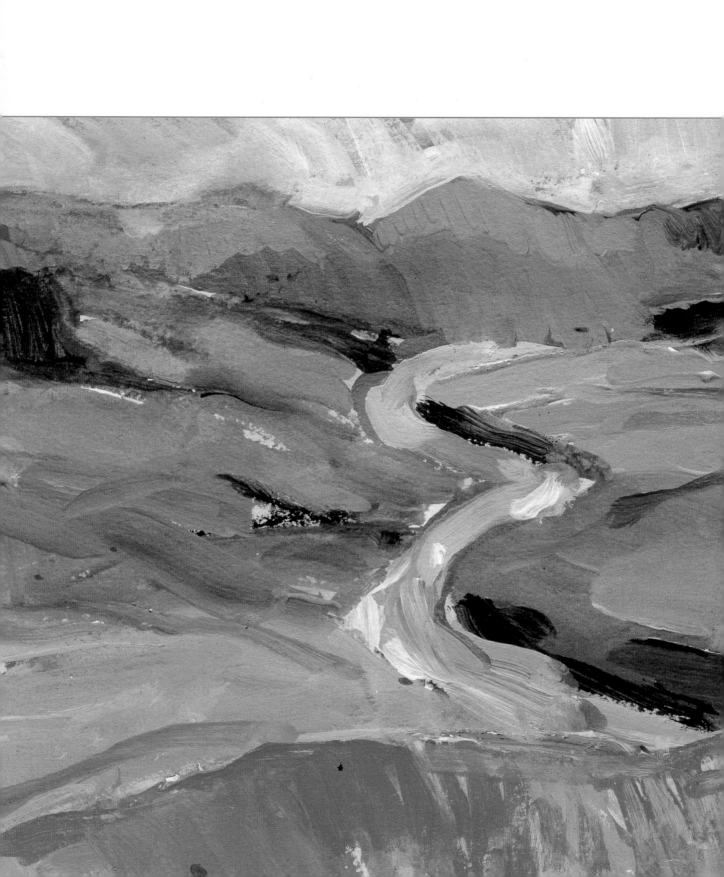

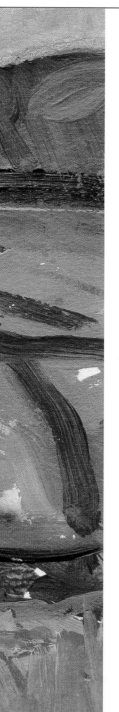

The SEDUCTIVENESS *of* NATURE

Of all the favourite subjects of artists, landscape is one of the most beloved, especially among amateur artists. However, painting landscape as an autonomous, freestanding subject is a fairly recent development in the history of art. The importance of landscape painting increased throughout the twentieth century.

This interest can be explained in several ways, but landscape's main attraction is its intrinsic beauty, its grand scale, its variability, its shapes, colours and textures that move us so deeply. For modern-day people, nature is an escape from a grey, industrialized society, a return to our origins. Painting landscapes means discovering the natural environment. This book takes a more basic approach than that of the romantic painters of the eighteenth century, who looked for the fantastic and the exotic in nature.

In modern society, considerable time is devoted to leisure, and as the speed of transportation increases at a dizzying rate, so does our geographic mobility. Some artists use depictions of landscape to record travel experiences and discover new places.

However, this genre cannot be understood in isolation. Landscape is a universal theme; an ideal framework for human activity. Throughout the history of art, landscape has, with good reason, often taken on historic, symbolic and psychological elements – that is, landscape includes many of the themes that usually are found in other genres.

Another aspect of landscape that fascinates painters is the metamorphosis that it under-goes with the weather and the passage of time: a day, the seasons. A large part of landscape painting's effect lies in how it depicts the interaction between the eternal shapes of the earth and the transitory effects of the weather.

For beginners, landscape is the best genre for starting to paint because it does not require a great deal of academic knowledge or mastery of the strict rules of drawing.

The purpose of this book is to introduce you to the fascinating artistic possibilities that emerge from the natural environment, to teach you the basic principles of representation and to allow you to begin painting landscapes confidently, boldly and without hesitation. With the desire to learn and constant practice, you will gain the skills necessary to paint a broad variety of landscapes. In landscape painting, you will discover a way to understand the nature of the earth – its greatness, its harshness and its beauty – and to find meaning in it.

SYNTHESIS

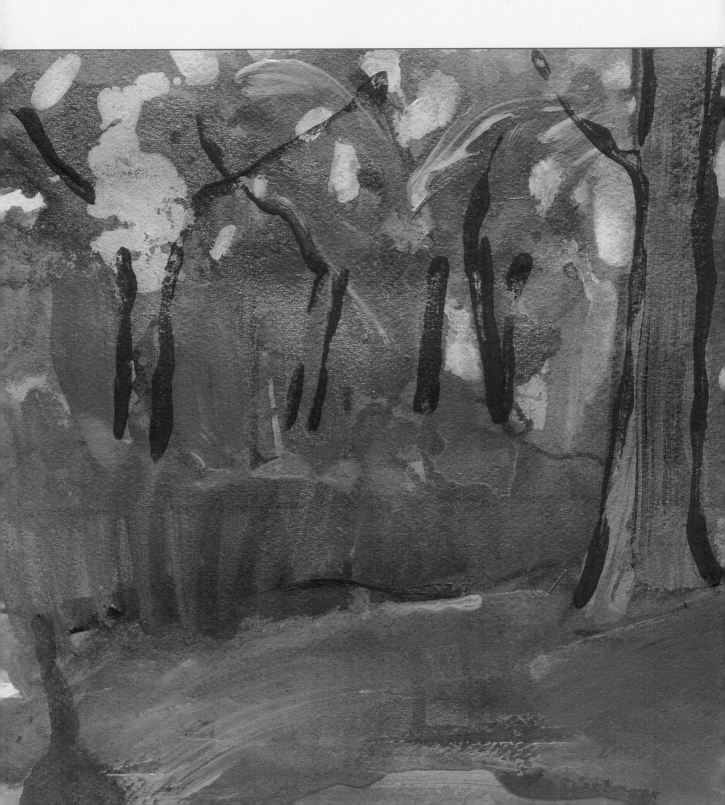

SYNTHESIS *and* RESOURCES
Interpretations of the LANDSCAPE

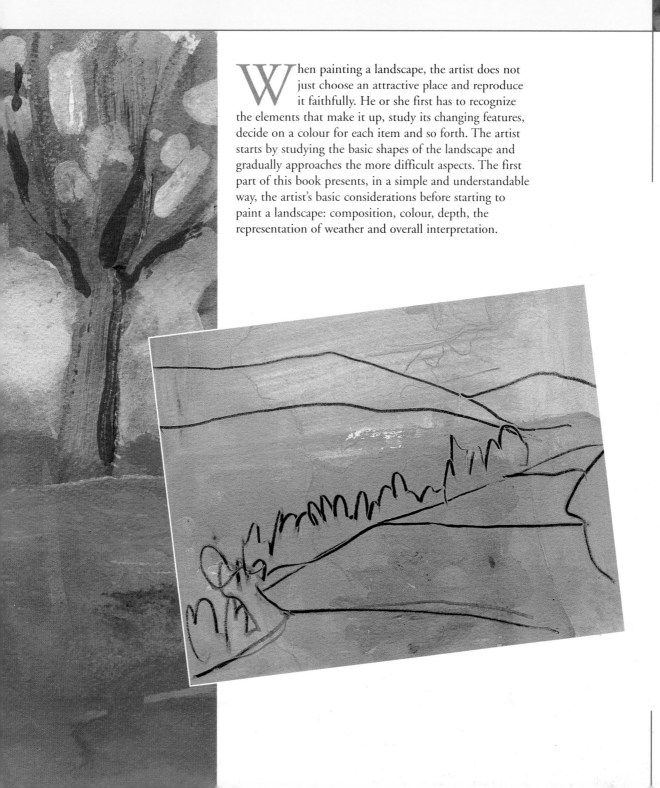

hen painting a landscape, the artist does not just choose an attractive place and reproduce it faithfully. He or she first has to recognize the elements that make it up, study its changing features, decide on a colour for each item and so forth. The artist starts by studying the basic shapes of the landscape and gradually approaches the more difficult aspects. The first part of this book presents, in a simple and understandable way, the artist's basic considerations before starting to paint a landscape: composition, colour, depth, the representation of weather and overall interpretation.

From Sketch to LANDSCAPE

From Sketch to LANDSCAPE

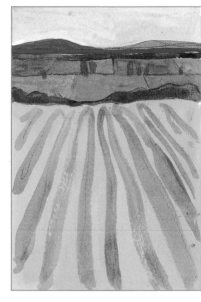

All the shapes of nature can be reduced to a few schematic lines. Sketching involves roughly laying out the main features of a landscape on paper. Preparatory sketches, no matter how small or rudimentary, are always useful because they stimulate objective observation and help determine the character of the composition.

An elevated horizon de-emphasizes the sky and focuses attention on the ground.

Synthesising Planes

Before starting to paint, the artist synthesises the landscape with a few decisive lines that provide structure to the main composition and the landmarks. The lines should also define the planes. The sketch must be geometric and minimalist, without details or complex shapes.

A few lines are all it takes to locate the main features.

Curves contribute rhythm to the composition and reflect the shapes in nature.

The Law of Curvature

The principle of this law is that all natural shapes are based on curves rather than straight lines. As a result, in order to achieve a good composition, it is necessary for the lines to be curved rather than straight or angular, as much as possible.

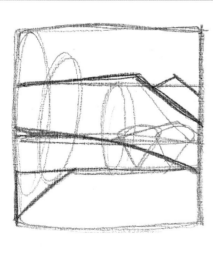

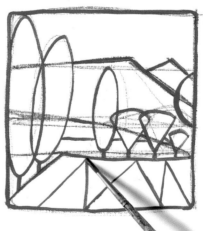

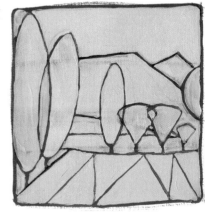

When sketching a landscape, try to identify geometric shapes that allow you to sketch the outlines of the composition.

Then synthesise the various planes using diagonal straight lines; the fields and mountains are represented with triangular shapes.

By recognizing these basic shapes in nature, you can create either a preliminary sketch ready for painting or a finished work with flat areas of colour.

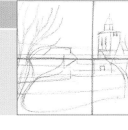

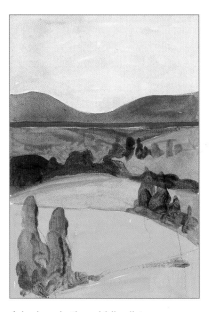

A horizon in the middle distance provides balance between the landmarks.

The Horizon Line

The horizon, where the earth meets the sky, is so basic to our experience of landscape that an abstract painting can be transformed into a landscape merely by dividing it with a horizontal line. Thus, the first line you need to make is the horizon line.

Tip

One way to make sketching easier is to first draw a horizontal and a vertical line that divide the canvas into four quadrants. This helps in locating the centre of the picture and the rest of the elements in the proper quadrants.

An Elevated Horizon

Elevated horizons tend to minimize the sky and emphasize the extension of the landscape. They lend themselves to a descriptive style that individualizes every feature of the terrain. For very flat landscapes, an elevated horizon is often the best choice.

A Medium Horizon

Placing the horizon in the middle of the picture creates a greater balance between the nearest and farthest planes. It is best to avoid dividing the paper into two even halves. Instead place the line slightly above or below the midpoint of the paper.

A low horizon emphasizes the sky; this is an ideal choice for working with clouds.

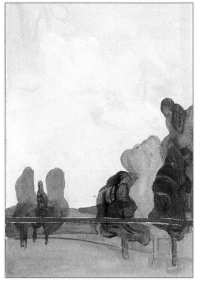

A Low Horizon

A low horizon line allows for few landmarks, you don't have far to go before you reach the sky. The features located in the foreground take on a more monumental appearance.

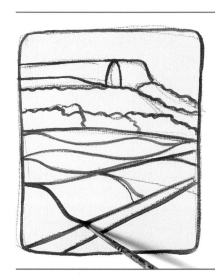

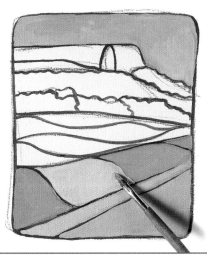

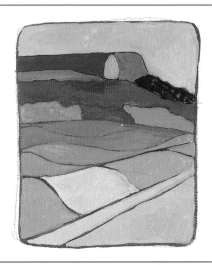

In the previous exercise you learned how to synthesise shapes, and in this one you will learn how to proceed with colours. Start with a line sketch similar to the previous one.

Fill in each segment using the dominant colour of the actual model.

Apply the colours flat to achieve a chromatic approximation of the real model. This will give you a better understanding of how the colours function.

SYNTHESISING COLOURS

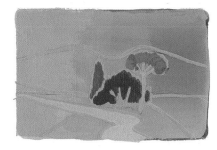

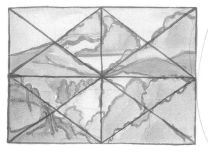

Grouping all the elements of the landscape in the centre of the painting creates an excessively symmetrical and static composition.

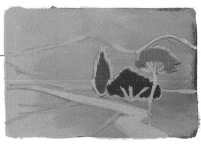

FORMATS,
Framing, and Templates

Paintings can be described as open windows to an imaginary world, but artists sometimes forget this when making preliminary sketches. When you paint, you can alter, adapt or reorganize the format and the framing of the landscape; there is no rule that requires including something simply because it is there.

It is a good idea to offset the subject of the landscape to one side to create a more interesting composition.

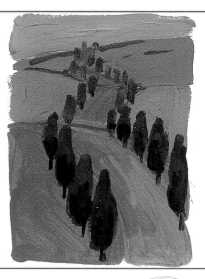

Lorrain's template makes it possible to compose a landscape in a very orderly fashion.

Lorrain's Template

Lorrain's template, a system developed by the French landscape painter Claude Lorrain, consists of a rectangle divided by diagonal lines that cross one another regularly. By adapting the landscape to this scheme, you can create a very harmonious composition.

Avoiding the Centre

It is not advisable to situate the focal point of the landscape in the centre of the painting, where the observer's gaze is first directed; offsetting it a little to one side balances the visual attraction and adds interest.

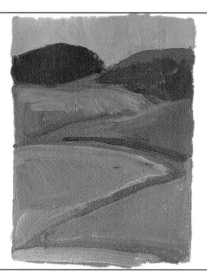

Every landscape must have a rhythm that activates the shapes and adds movement to an immobile scene. This is accomplished through the repetition of a motif, such as trees that line a road.

You can create rhythm by introducing a line that leads the gaze through different planes of the painting. An example is this red road that crosses the landscape.

Repetitive brushstrokes oriented in the same direction create a rhythmic surface and give the shapes a more dynamic appearance.

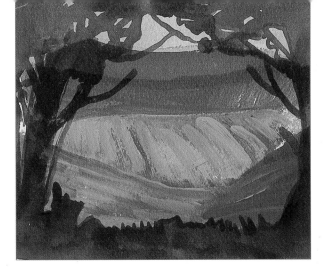

You can create one frame inside another by enclosing the landscape with a few trees located in the foreground. This technique highlights the depth of the painting.

Framing

One basic rule for framing is that the picture should contain a limited number of elements clearly differentiated by their tone, shape and size. To choose an effective frame, it is essential to distance yourself from the landscape to get a grasp on its various facets. A broad panorama without too many visual obstacles allows the artist to decide with greater clarity just what its most attractive feature is.

One Frame Inside Another

If you want to direct the observer's gaze to the back of the painting, you can use the traditional technique of creating a frame with a group of trees located in the foreground. This effect heightens the sensation of space; the foliage in the crown of the trees draws them toward the front of the composition and makes the mountains seem farther away. This inner frame surrounds the centre of the composition, drawing attention to the centre of interest.

Tip

The format of the work depends on the landscape. Isolated motifs (trees, buildings and so on) are often treated most effectively using vertical framing, but landscape framing is better suited to broad, deep panoramas.

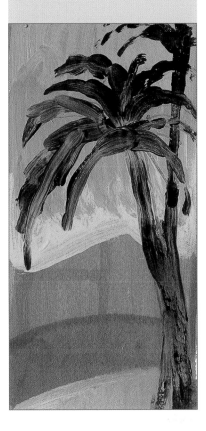

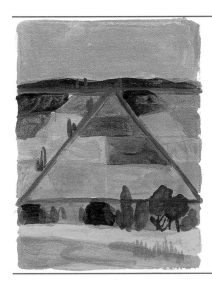

People prefer compositions based on geometric schemes. When it comes to framing, it is best to use a scheme that corresponds to a precise geometric shape.

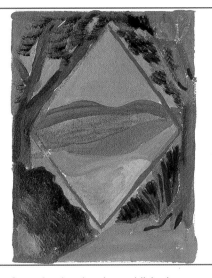

Once the rhombus is established as the basis for the composition, all the elements that make up the landscape must conform to it.

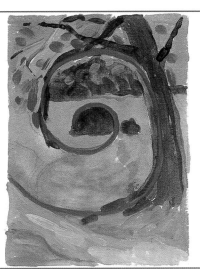

Spiral shapes are less static, and they lead the observer's gaze straight to the centre of the painting. This scheme is perfect for creating trees in sinuous shapes.

GEOMETRICAL SCHEMES

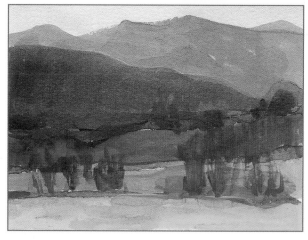

Warm colours predominate in the foreground, whereas cold ones define the most distant planes.

Working in Different
PLANES

A landscape is constructed by first superimposing the main planes that make it up. Every plane is represented by a certain colour and treatment. Before beginning to paint, you must decide which plane presents the greatest visual interest. Then you must target that area of the painting and organize the remainder around it.

Working in Planes

Space can be represented by dividing it into planes. Planes are divisions in space where items located at about the same distance from the eye are grouped together. To create depth, planes are overlapped, indicating to the observer which one is in front of the other.

Close and Distant Colours

The effect of superimposing planes can be heightened by painting the closest planes in warm colours and the most distant ones in cold colours. Warm colours (yellow, orange, red and carmine) bring the planes closer to the observer; cold colours (blue, green and violet) move them farther away. It is difficult to get this colour scheme to work in a landscape, but it is a valuable concept to think about.

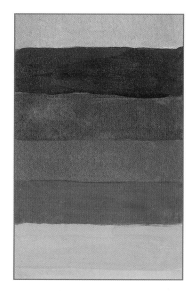

Using an ordered succession of colours, you can highlight the effect of distance in the landscape.

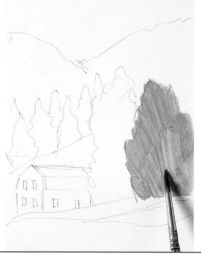

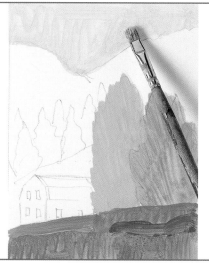

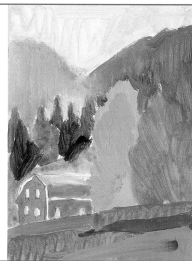

When confronting a blank canvas, the first impulse of every beginner is to cover it quickly. Begin by painting every area with its approximate colour.

Cover the canvas with uniform colours, focusing on the trees in the foreground and the sky. Work quickly and with fairly dilute paint.

You can finish the initial colouring in a matter of a few minutes. This will serve as a base for the next layers of colour.

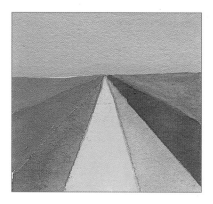

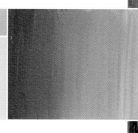

Diagonal lines create distance in the landscape. All it takes is a few lines oriented toward the same point on the horizon.

Tip

It is a good idea to practice gradations, which are very useful in representing the effect of light on each plane of the landscape.

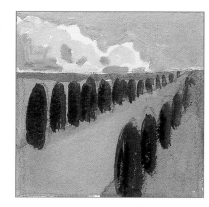

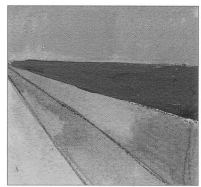

When using diagonal lines to produce the effect of receding space, it is more convincing to draw them from left to right, the same direction in which we read.

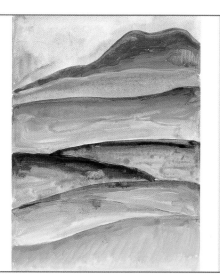

Diagonal Lines in Landscapes

The effect of perspective is easy to create if a clear diagonal orders the features of the landscape from the foreground into the distance. In such cases it is not necessary to create perspective through additional effects because the depth is already indicated clearly enough.

Ways Into and Through a Painting

In a landscape with superimposed planes, you must not let the paint get too flat so you can open up routes that allow the viewer to penetrate into the scene. There are many ways to direct the gaze

toward the interior of the space and into the depth of a painting. In a landscape, a road or a river that leads toward the horizon is a route through the image.

The Direction of the View

The effect of distance in a landscape is more convincing if it coincides with the direction in which we read. For example, if you are going to place a tree in the foreground, it is natural to use the left edge of the paper so that the viewer's gaze advances in depth toward more distant planes in the landscape.

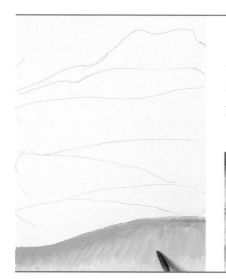

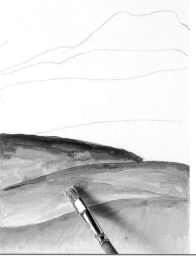

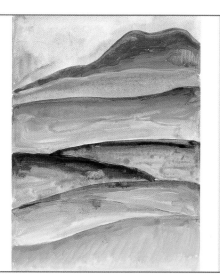

Practise painting the different planes using gradations. This effect is very appropriate for both colourist treatments and realistic interpretations.

Paint each strip of colour using a slight gradation – a line of saturated, dark colour at the top that gradually lightens as it descends.

White can be used to form a gradation by diluting the colours; a lighter shade of the same colour can also be used. This treatment rounds the planes and appears to give them more volume.

PAINTING PLANES WITH COLOUR GRADATIONS

13

Harmonizing COLOUR

Harmonizing COLOUR *in Landscape*

Harmonizing colour involves painting with a certain colour range. The artist's mission is to recognize the chromatic tendencies that exist in nature and to select the proper harmonious colour range. This means organizing the colours on your palette to produce the colour ranges required in each case.

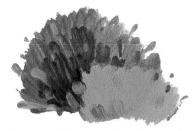

Mixing green with other nearby colours in the chromatic circle (ochres, browns, blues and yellow) produces a variety of shades.

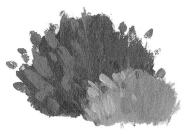

Combine different shades of green to represent a cluster of vegetation.

Painting the Green of the Landscape

When painting a landscape, don't allow your eyes to be deceived by items of similar colours. It is appropriate to exaggerate colour variations to make the various elements of the landscape clearly discernible. A painting that contains nothing but greens and colours related to green quickly becomes boring. To avoid this, introduce little touches of other colours that contrast with the green without disrupting the balance (greenish blue or yellow). If you want greater chromatic contrast, reds, oranges and even purples can be added among the greens to provide variety.

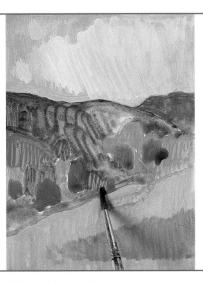

If you want greater chromatic variety, you can superimpose small touches of other colours onto the green. It is not always necessary to use green in painting a green landscape.

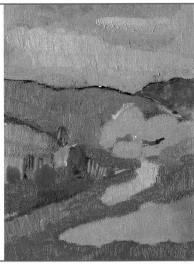

A harmonious painting can be transformed by experimenting with bold contrasts. Let's begin with a composition in a harmonious range of cold colours.

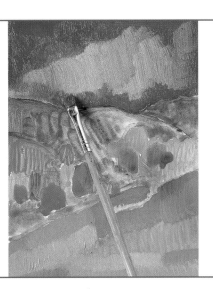

Over the base of bluish colours, the sky is painted in red and the foreground in yellow, intentionally breaking the chromatic harmony. The landscape is completely transformed.

The preceding situation can be corrected by painting the sky in yellow and covering the foreground with red. Notice how this improves the result.

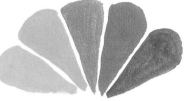

The range of warm colours consists of yellow, orange, red and their derivatives.

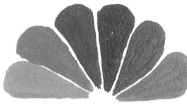

The range of cold colours is made up mainly of blues, greens and their mixtures with other colours.

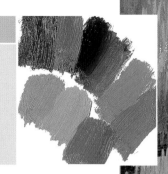

Tip

To paint a landscape, it is not necessary to buy every colour available. Quite the contrary. It is necessary to know how to mix select colours accurately so that each one can be used in its entire range of tone and intensity.

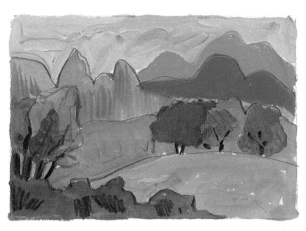

A tree painted in red on a background dominated by greens and blues turns into a centre of interest.

The Centre of Interest

It is commonly said that every landscape must have a centre of interest, or a focal point, like a visual invitation that attracts the observer's gaze. Traditionally, the focal point is located in a middle plane of the landscape, with some elements in the foreground.

The Range of Warm Colours

The range of warm colours is made up of red and its derivatives, because red is considered the colour that contains the greatest warmth. It is well suited for the foreground, sunsets and landscapes depicting intense heat.

The Range of Cold Colours

The range of cold colours is made up of blue and its derivatives. It begins with green and ends with bluish violet. It is the best colour range for painting distant planes, cloudy days and cold winter landscapes.

The Range of Broken Colours

The range of broken colours is produced by mixing complementary colours in unequal proportions with white. Broken colours are suited to most kinds of representation, but they may be inappropriate for very sunny landscapes that need lots of colour and strong contrasts between light and shadow.

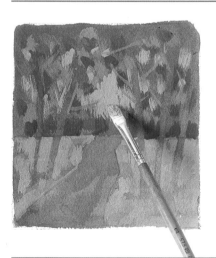

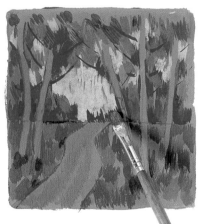

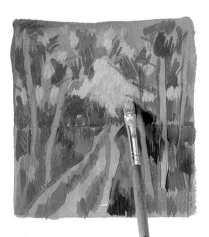

Look at this example of a forest painted in different chromatic ranges. Warm colours such as reds and yellows appear to give off heat.

This forest is constructed using cold colours derived from greens and blues. They give the composition a much more wintry appearance, and the scene appears more somber.

The broken colour scale is made up of greyed or broken colours that give the whole composition a harmonious appearance.

LANDSCAPES IN HARMONIOUS COLOUR RANGES

The effect of perspective is achieved by directing the diagonals of the landscape toward a single point on the horizon line.

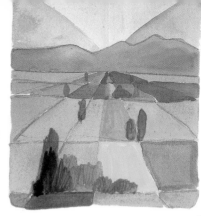

The Appearance *of* DEPTH

The sense of three-dimensional space is a notable element in landscape painting. An understanding of perspective makes it easier to create the appearance of depth in a landscape. You can also create a perspective without lines, using contrast and definition in the foreground and muted colours in the more distant planes.

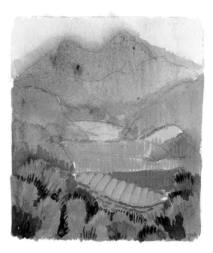

Atmospheric Effect

In the more distant planes of a landscape, the colours take on bluish or violet tones. This is an optical illusion caused by water vapour and particles of dust in the air that soften the shapes and colours in the distance to create a mist.

Perspective

The artist's most important device for creating depth is perspective. If you select the proper vanishing point or arrange the features of the landscape in a certain way, viewers are prompted to direct their gaze from the foreground to the background.

As the planes become more distant, they appear more discoloured and out of focus.

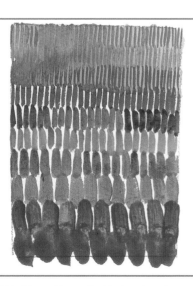

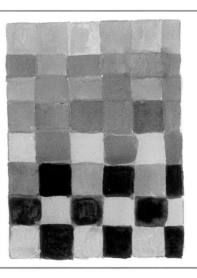

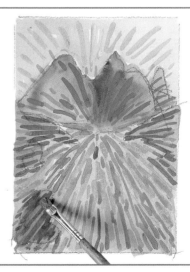

Working with small, thin brushstrokes in the background and thick, dense ones in the foreground, you can create an effect of distance.

Contrasts among colours are much more pronounced in the foreground; they are softened and may be scarcely perceptible in the more distant planes.

For a more expressive effect, you can make all the brushstrokes in the landscape converge toward a single point located on the horizon line. This is called the vanishing point.

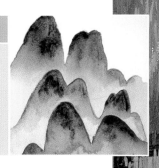

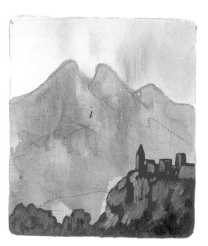

Plenty of contrast in the foreground and a vague background help to indicate the distances in a landscape.

Tip

In Chinese painting, a watery atmosphere dissolves the base of the distant mountains. Thus, the peaks float in the sky while the base disappears entirely.

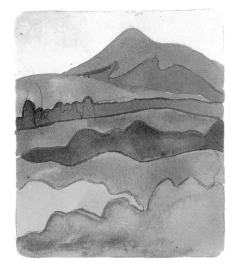

In the coulisse *effect, depth is produced by juxtaposing various strips of uniform colour in an orderly fashion.*

An Empty Background

Usually, the foreground of a landscape is clearly visible, but you must guess or deduce the shapes in the distance. Although the atmosphere hides the shapes, you can see enough to work out what they are. This is precisely what a landscape painter does in leaving empty areas without detail: The voids aid in creating a sense of distance.

Contrast in the Foreground

If an element of familiar proportions (such as trees, cars or boulders) is located in the foreground, the observer will be able to compare the dimensions of the near object with the ones located in more distant planes. The colours in the foreground are intense, the textures very noticeable and the outlines clearly defined. A mist blurs the outlines in the more distant planes.

The *Coulisse* Effect

In French the word *coulisse* is used to designate the curtains and theatrical decorations that span the stage from side to side. This term also describes a composition that simulates the effect of depth by juxtaposing successive planes, similar to curtains in flat colours.

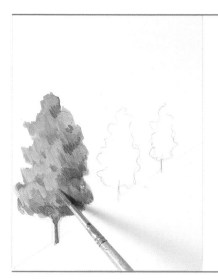

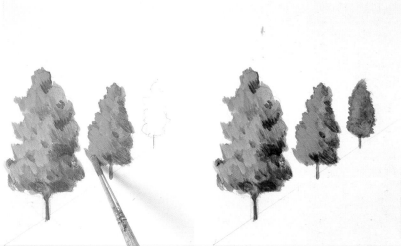

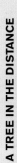

A TREE IN THE DISTANCE

To paint a tree located in the foreground you have to differentiate clearly between the light areas and the shaded ones, add the texture of the leaves and include a few details.

When this same tree is located in a middle plane, the brushstrokes disappear, and you distinguish the shaded area from the lighter one with even colour fields.

A tree located in a distant plane is rendered as little more than a field of colour with minimal differentiation. The distance doesn't allow us to see details, and the shaded areas are scarcely distinguished from the lighter ones.

17

Clear skies are commonly presented using a gradation.

The Importance of the SKY

The Importance of the SKY

Even though the sky is changeable and unpredictable, it is extremely important because it determines the overall nature of a landscape. It acts as a huge window that inundates everything with its light and sets the chromatic scheme, determining the colours that will appear in the painting.

Clear Skies

It is not advisable to paint a clear sky uniformly. Avoid the impression of uniformity by creating a vibration of light and colour.

In addition to general harmony, a gradation produces a convincing sensation of light. In a clear sky, the colour tends to be more intense at the top (where the blue is more saturated) and slightly lighter toward the horizon, sometimes with a mild tendency toward a yellowish-cream shade.

The Shape of Clouds

It is important to pay close attention to the shape of the clouds so that they melt naturally into the surrounding atmosphere. The clouds should not be outlined clearly: it is best to let some outlines stand out from the background and others blend in with it.

Clouds should have vaguely defined outlines that stand out in some areas and are blurred by shading and gradations in others.

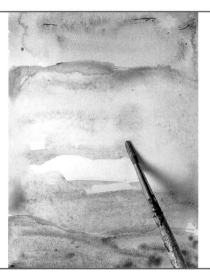

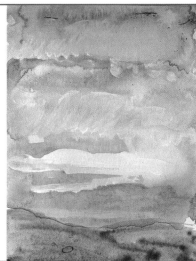

There are two basic ways to paint the sky, one of which involves using washes. Allow thinly diluted paint to flow onto the paper so that the colours blend together randomly.

Using a round brush, apply violet washes over the still-wet blue wash; the new washes mix immediately with the underlying colour to form gradations.

With a wet wash, add new colours that will blend in. When these are dry, use white brushstrokes to suggest the shapes of the clouds.

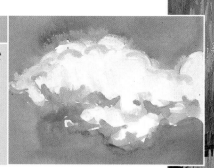

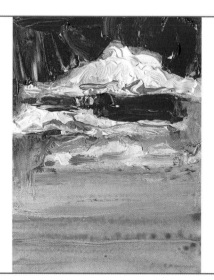

Tip

Amateur artists often commit the error of rounding clouds so that they appear solid and angular, like piles of rocks placed in a sack. Clouds should not appear solid or lumpy.

As clouds approach the horizon, they appear more elongated, and their yellowish or violet base blends slightly with the blue of the sky.

Perspective in Clouds

The laws of atmospheric perspective apply to clouds just as they do to landscapes. Because of the effect of perspective, clouds appear more intense and warm when they are high in the sky, and as they approach the horizon their outlines soften and they take on a bluish colour. Their shapes also change; they appear smaller and flatter in the distance. The furthest clouds often blend with the mist of the horizon.

An Explosion of Colour

The sky often takes on colours other than blue. A sky can be pink, golden, yellow, orange or greenish, depending on the time of day. This effect is a good one to keep in mind, since the light produced by specific weather conditions determines the general tone of the work. Typically, the most dramatic chromatic effects are seen at sunset.

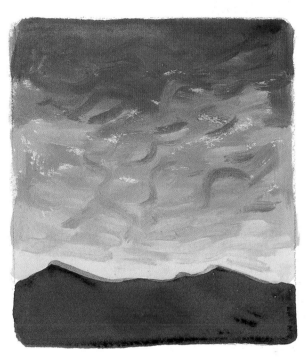

Sunsets are a perfect theme for giving free rein to colour and brushstrokes.

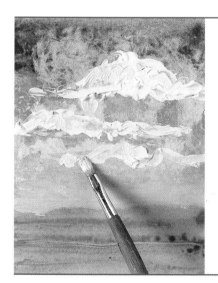

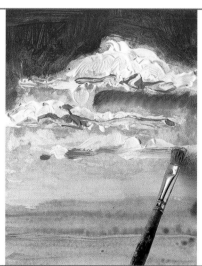

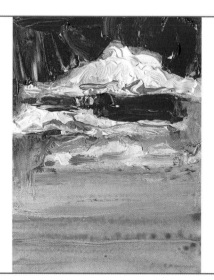

Impasto gives the sky a very expressive appearance. Begin by using lots of paint on the brush and applying the white of the clouds over a sky created with a wash.

Highlight the sky with a darker blue, taking care to avoid colouring over the clouds. Paint the shadow at the bottom of each cloud using striated brushstrokes in violet.

Using a palette knife and ultramarine blue, paint the upper part of the sky in a contrasting blue. The point of the palette knife drags part of the white from the cloud upward into the sky.

SKY WITH IMPASTO

19

NATURAL
SHAPES

The NATURAL SHAPES
of Vegetation

Vegetation makes up a major part of many landscapes. It is noteworthy for its varied textures. In addition, if it is painted from a close vantage point, it provides a fascinating richness of detail and colour variations.

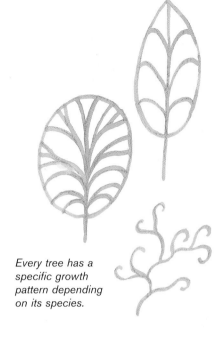

Every tree has a specific growth pattern depending on its species.

Growth Patterns

Regardless of how strange the structure of a tree may appear, it can be simplified into a basic geometric shape. There is a well-defined logic and order to plant growth, which can be synthesised with rhythmic or spiral progressions. When plants grow, they don't extend their branches randomly; the branches share a strong, single impulse, as if released from a nozzle. Each branch follows a certain path at the same time that it makes up an outer curve, the character and proportions of which are peculiar to each plant species.

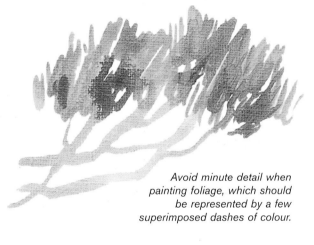

Avoid minute detail when painting foliage, which should be represented by a few superimposed dashes of colour.

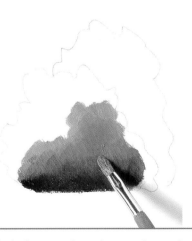

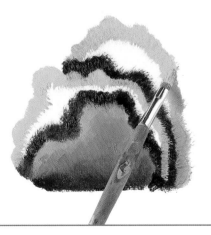

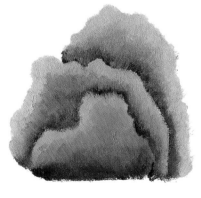

To depict vegetation using superimposed layers, apply the gradation effect. This keeps the various planes from blending with one another.

The top part of each crown is done in yellow and the lower part in a fairly dark green so that each plant shape stands out against a darker background.

Use soft transitions from yellow to green to create gradations in the strips of colour. Thus, the yellow stands out in contrast to the darker green of the foliage behind it.

It is crucial to learn how to synthesise the shape of trees using economical brushstrokes and colour.

Tip

A few details add up to a lot. To paint a branch full of leaves, paint the shape of the whole and then highlight three individual leaves. The eye does the rest.

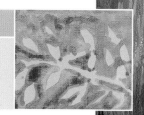

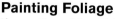

With distance, vegetation becomes blurry, indistinct and slightly faded.

Painting Foliage

If you attempt to paint each leaf of a tree, you will invariably produce an image with no vitality. Painting leaves and other details of plants demands quick, careful work, with few details and little refinement of what has already been painted. The texture of the foliage is produced through smooth, pronounced brushstrokes that simulate the movement of the leaves. The leaves appear at uneven intervals and grow smaller as they get further away from their base or origin. You must look for the basic shapes that make up the clusters of leaves and the changes in foliage density.

Vegetation and Distance

A plant in the distance appears as nothing more than a flat blotch of green; along with other blotches, it makes up a pleasant cluster that adds colour to the landscape. A distant tree is not a fragment of flat, uniform colour, but rather a globular mass of soft or velvety texture, partially veiled in a misty vagueness.

Learning to Synthesise

In drawing trees, it is advisable to use the technique of synthesis, which involves painting with fewer lines – just the necessary ones – and checking the model with half-closed eyes to eliminate unnecessary details. It is not possible to paint a tree if you try to depict every mark, hollow, crack, bit of texture, and so forth.

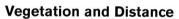

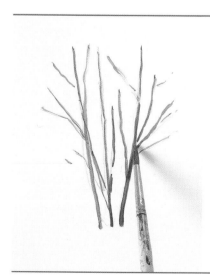

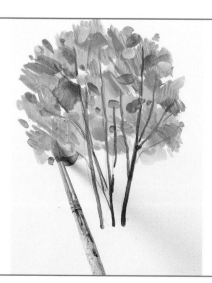

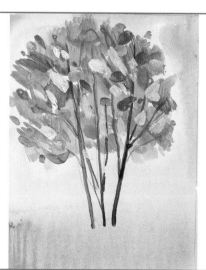

FOUR SPOTS ARE ALL IT TAKES

To paint a tree, you merely need to suggest it with a few brushstrokes. Let's look at an example. Using a fine, round brush, paint the trunk and the branches in dark brown.

Next we paint the leaves with small spots of superimposed yellow and red. Their shape must be imprecise, and they must vary in size.

Once the blotches are dry, apply brushstrokes in white that simulate the passage of light among the leaves. Paint the background in ochre. This tree was created in scarcely two minutes.

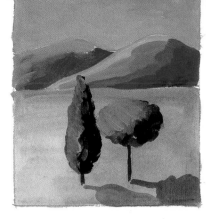

Lateral light

LIGHT *in* Landscape

LIGHT
in Landscape

Overhead light

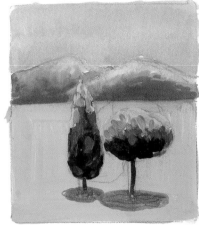

As the day progresses, a landscape is subjected to different light, which varies according to the position of the sun and the atmospheric conditions. It is worthwhile to understand these factors, especially how variations in the position and intensity of the universal light source − the sun − affect the landscape.

Lateral Light

Lateral light occurs when the sun strikes the landscape from the side and from a fairly low point in the sky. Sharp contrasts between light and dark reveal the shape and texture of the landscape and offer a broad range of descriptive shadows that help define the areas surrounding the objects. The parts of the vegetation that face the light source are illuminated.

Overhead Light

Overhead light is when the sun is located at its highest point in the sky. The violent brightness of the midday sun shrinks the long shadows characteristic of lateral light. The lightest and warmest areas of the tableau are the shapes that form a right angle with the light.

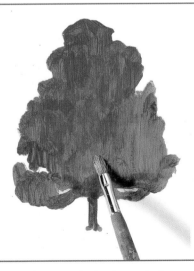

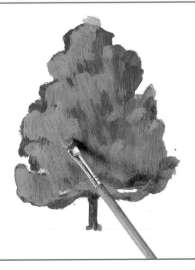

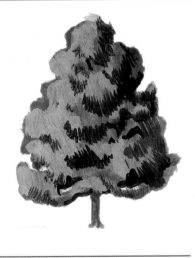

Many features of a landscape invite treatment as three-dimensional shapes, which have their own volume. To highlight the shape of a tree, first paint it with a flat green.

Use a yellowish green to paint the illuminated areas of the leaves in an impressionistic manner. This highlights the volume of the tree.

Paint the shaded areas, distributing the contrasts in such a way that some parts of the landscape advance outward while others recede into the background.

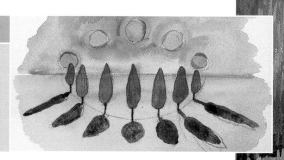

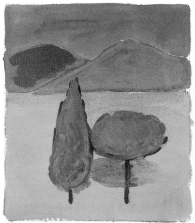

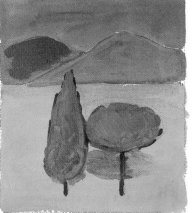

Frontal light

Frontal Light

Frontal light comes from behind the artist and causes the sky to appear darker. The foreground of the image is seen most clearly and its tones deepen and cool off as the shapes recede into the distance. The shadows are hidden behind the features that make up the landscape.

Diffuse Light

Because of the filtering effect of clouds, diffuse light reaches objects in an evenly sifted fashion. In these conditions, the shadows appear softer, like dark, indistinct halos created with blends and gradations.

Tip

Shadows from sunlight move with the sun; this means that the shape and the length of the shadows vary with the passage of the daylight hours.

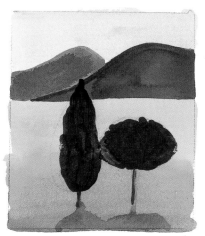

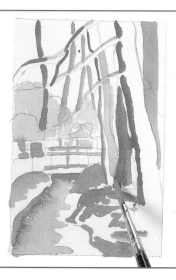

Diffuse light

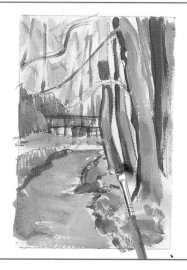

Backlighting

Backlighting

In a backlit scene, the light reaches the model from behind and shades the planes visible to the artist. The sky in the scene is the brightest area. Backlighting reduces the features of the landscape to a series of dark shadows that stand out as silhouettes. The tone of the ground lightens as it approaches the horizon.

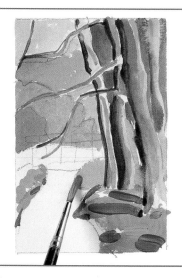

The tonal value of shadows is commonly brown − that is, a shade similar to the feature represented but mixed with a little black, brown or grey.

Since the shadows appear to have a temperature opposite that of the light source, they can also be painted in blue.

A more colourist treatment creates a greater chromatic impact. Instead of working with cold, subdued colours, try painting the shadows in red.

THE COLOUR OF SHADOWS

23

The CHALLENGE of CLOUDS

Much of the attraction of clouds stems from the voluptuous shapes they take on. Cumulus clouds appear solid, have volume and owe much of their majesty to the sun, which illuminates them and gives them their characteristic shape. Painting clouds involves synthesising, abbreviating, improvising and imagining; it is really an exercise in interpretation, a way of transforming nature using shapes and colours. Let's see how to paint a sky filled with storm clouds.

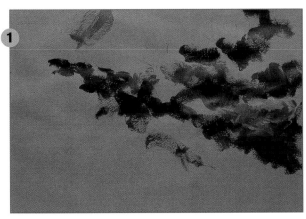

1. Working on a blue canvas, sketch a few fine lines in pencil. Use a deep purple to paint with agitated strokes.

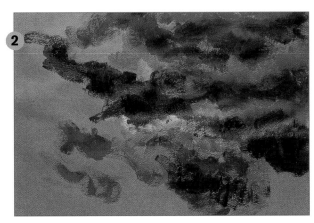

2. Leave some small areas where the intermediate tone of the original blue is visible. Use white sparingly to introduce the first light areas.

3. The last additions of colour are in bluish and pinkish violet with lots of grey. Juxtaposed brushstrokes of these colours give body to the clouds that completely cover the sky.

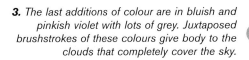

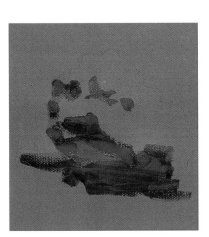

Inexperienced painters should not trust to improvisation; it is a better idea to first draw the shape of the cloud in pencil. Beginners should also spend a few moments studying the direction of the light and paint the shadow in a shade of violet.

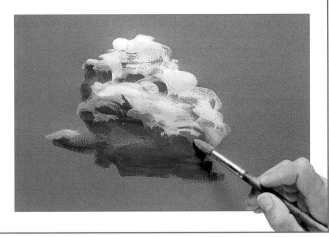

Paint the body of the cloud by adding white with very quick brushstrokes similar to small, curving whiplashes. The white takes over the upper part of the cloud and fuses with the violet in the intermediate zone.

PAINTING TREES

Trees located in a near plane can be created using a series of brushstrokes or impasto. It is crucial to control the direction of each brushstroke. Study these three examples done in oil. This is an opaque medium that makes it possible to redo and retouch using light colours over dark ones. That quality makes oil ideal for painting the crown of these trees without fear of making mistakes.

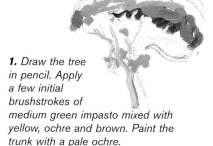

1. Draw the tree in pencil. Apply a few initial brushstrokes of medium green impasto mixed with yellow, ochre and brown. Paint the trunk with a pale ochre.

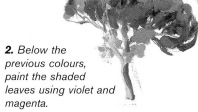

2. Below the previous colours, paint the shaded leaves using violet and magenta.

3. Apply the final touches with a finer brush. Pay particular attention to the branches illuminated by the sun; they appear orange.

1. In a palm tree the trunk takes on great importance. After doing the initial sketch, trace the trunk's curvature using slightly orange sienna and a firm brushstroke. Paint the first leaves using short brushstrokes in the shape of a comma.

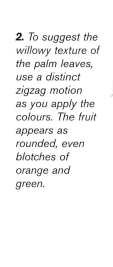

2. To suggest the willowy texture of the palm leaves, use a distinct zigzag motion as you apply the colours. The fruit appears as rounded, even blotches of orange and green.

3. Finish up the palm tree by using burnt umber to darken the top of the trunk. Complete the foliage with brushstrokes of purplish paint that are much less precise than the previous ones.

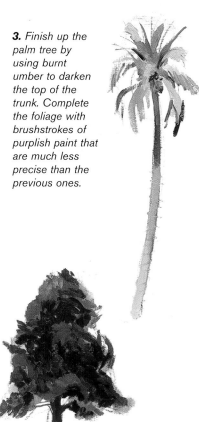

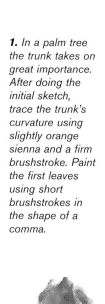

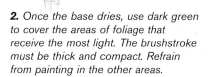

1. Cover the crown of the tree with ochre paint mixed with turpentine, then add green and a touch of red to form gradations. The trunk is painted in burnt umber.

2. Once the base dries, use dark green to cover the areas of foliage that receive the most light. The brushstroke must be thick and compact. Refrain from painting in the other areas.

3. Finish the darkest areas of the tree with burnt umber. The new brushstrokes are more agitated than the previous ones, and they leave small light areas.

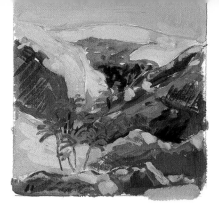

The effect of sunlight on the landscape is created by heightening the contrast of the shadows.

Weather CONDITIONS

Climatic conditions determine the appearance of the landscape by imparting transitory effects. The weather infuses the landscape with life and character, and everything that suggests immobility, stability and solidity in nature disappears.

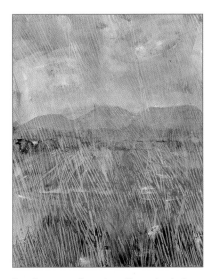

Sunlight

The presence of shadows is an important part of depicting a landscape bathed in strong sunlight. On sunny days there is greater contrast between the temperature changes; that is, the warm colours (in the sunlit areas) and the cold ones (in the shadows) are more lively and harmonize less with one another.

Painting Rain

In oils, a heavy rainfall can be indicated by making diagonal lines on the layer of paint with the point of a palette knife. A wash is commonly used to create an intense atmosphere that makes it hard to distinguish the outline of the landscape features. A few lines can then be added to suggest falling rain.

In oils or acrylics, the effect of rain is created by superimposing soft linear brushstrokes over the landscape.

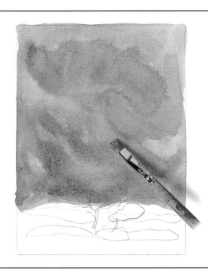

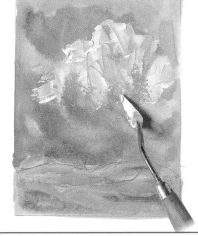

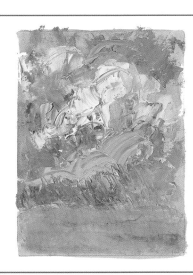

Creating a storm requires working quickly, using dynamic brushstrokes and expressive impastos. To begin, paint the sky using irregular washes in shades of violet.

Over a dried background, apply impastos of white paint using a spatula, with a more opaque white in the top of the cloud and a more transparent white in the lower part.

In new additions of impastos, randomly mix in red, blue, violet and white. Use the point of the palette knife to add sgraffito, heightening the dynamic effect.

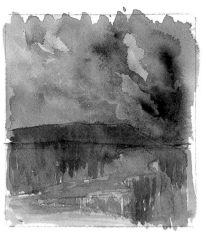

Stormy skies are dominated by greys and violets, and they darken the colours of the landscape.

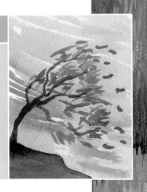

With a wash used to depict rain, diagonal brushstrokes only partially cover the background.

Foggy Weather

Fog or mist is depicted using delicate and nearly imperceptible effects, subdued colours and diffuse shapes that require a sensitive treatment. A landscape obscured by fog appears in gradations, with more precise shapes and broken colours in the foreground and nearly indistinguishable profiles and bleached colours in the background.

Stormy Weather

Storms can transform a peaceful place into a scene of drama and contrast. The violence and the speed that characterize storms are commonly expressed through lively, descriptive brushstrokes that reinforce the agitation in the landscape. As for the sky, storm clouds move at high speed and they should be painted quickly.

Snow

Snow reflects light and breaks up the ground into strong patterns of light and dark. On steep terrain it creates interesting shadows because it reflects the irregular contours of the land it covers. In painting snow, avoid infusing everything with white. Instead, create an illusion by shading white with blue, orange, pink and yellow. Since snow is white, it reflects sunlight in the lightest areas, and light from the sky in the shadows, thereby presenting different chromatic values. For example, in sunrises and sunsets, the light reflected by the snow is pink or orange.

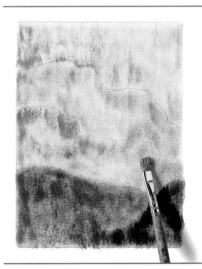

A dry brush is very appropriate for painting diffuse profiles and is an ideal tool for creating fog. Apply a different colour in each plane.

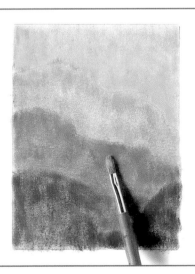

Over the original colours, add dry glazes that cover the white of the canvas more effectively.

The last passes with the brush are done using very washed-out colours that further unify each colour, avoiding excessive contrasts among the colours.

FOG WITH A DRY BRUSH

PAINTING SHADOWS

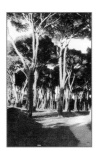

If you stop to analyze any landscape, you will see that its volume and shapes are the product of a combination of surfaces sculpted by light and shadow. The key for recreating the light involves reducing the effects of shadow on the landscape to four basic conditions. Let's look at a few examples.

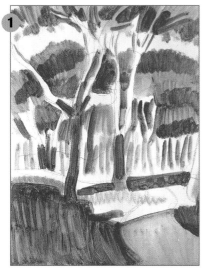

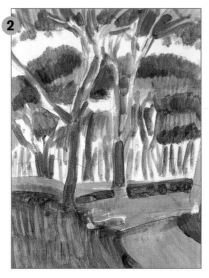

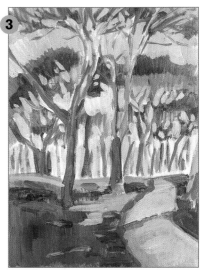

1. One traditional method involves first painting just the shadows with blue; the borders between light and shadow are created by defining the shaded areas with absolute precision.

2. As a foil to the bluish shadows, bright orange is added to cover the areas bathed in intense light. The indications of light serve not only to highlight, but also to provide an initial spatial impression of the landscape.

3. Reds, ochres and yellows are added in the illuminated areas, and blues and violets in the shaded ones. The representation of a shape in space depends on the relationship between warm and cold colours.

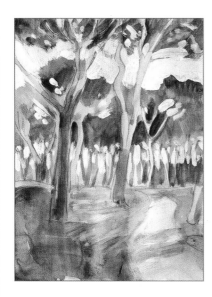

In a tonal approach, shading is done in brown, grey or black, and the colour of an object is gradually darkened without excessive contrast. Modeling and chiaroscuro effects can be useful with this technique.

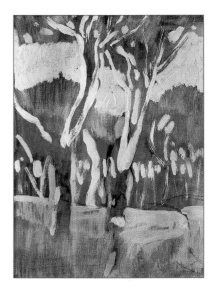

Another way to approach shadows is to paint the impression of the light with a pale ochre over a bluish background. The impression of the light depends on the contrasts. A sharp increase in the brightness of a colour is accepted as an indication of light.

COLOURS *in the* LANDSCAPE: *Communicating* ATMOSPHERE

Every landscape painting has a characteristic atmosphere determined by the interaction of colour and the artist's interpretation and treatment of the scene. When you paint a subject, try to capture the atmosphere and transmit the feelings of the place with chromatic keys. You can transmit the atmosphere – a sunny day, a sunset, a cold winter's day or a landscape under a hard rain – through colour and certain effects and brushstrokes.

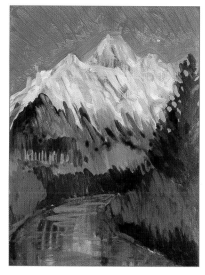

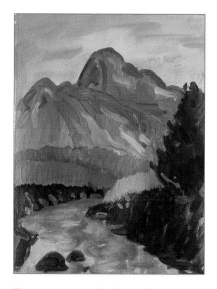

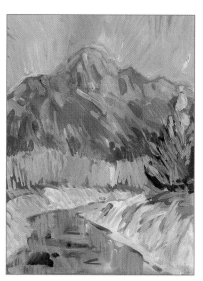

A sunny day can be depicted in a tonal manner, without excessive chromatic exaggeration. The colours of the vegetation are produced using various greens mixed with yellow and browns. The illuminated areas (mountain, vegetation and reflections in the water) are differentiated from the more shaded ones (the edge of the river and the fir tree on the right).

The sunset completely transforms the same landscape. It bathes the surfaces with a reddish light created with warm tones and fiery colours. The contrasts in the shaded areas along the edge of the river and the fir tree are darker, setting up a kind of backlighting.

Despite the orange reflections on the mountain from the sun dipping behind the horizon, the painting is completely dominated by blues and violets that communicate a sense of winter cold. A denser, more generous brushstroke helps represent the texture of the snow.

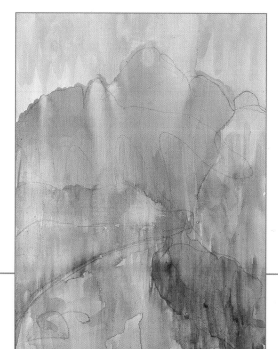

Because direct sunlight is the main colour activator, rainy days impart greyish colours to the landscape. The curtains of rain melt the colours and soften the outlines. The watery atmosphere allows us to see only a spectral image of the landscape. In such cases, working with washes is the best choice.

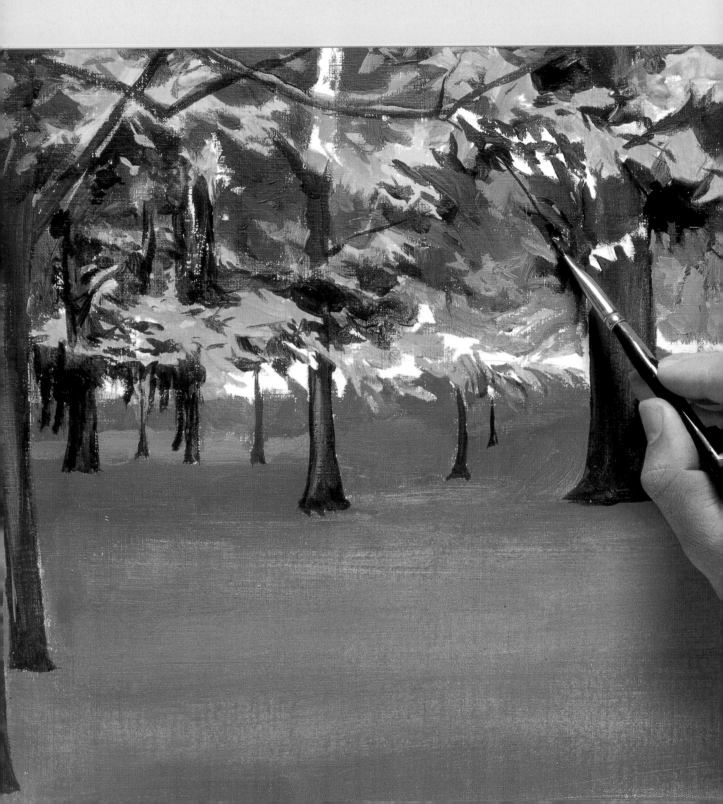

EXERCISES
PRACTICAL EXERCISES

In this section you will develop the basic techniques for successfully painting a natural landscape. You will learn how to represent vegetation located in different planes, use chromatic effects and create the impression of distance and atmosphere. You will see how the visual impression of the colours, the direction of the brushstrokes and the degree of definition combine to produce the desired effect. You will also practise a number of techniques and tricks that can be used to express the unique character of different landscapes.

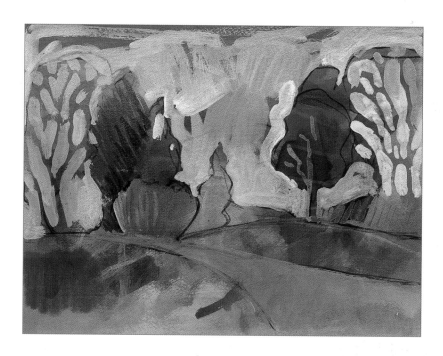

SYNTHETIC *Treatment* *of* LANDSCAPE

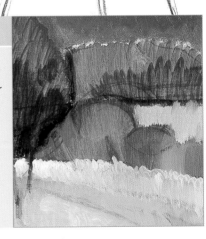

When using oil paints, it is possible to synthesise the shapes of the landscape perfectly with just a few areas of colour and practically no details. The shapes of the vegetation, although flat, are outlined and barely suggested by two or three superimposed tones. This method should be used for any landscape that requires a great degree of elaboration, especially because it allows for a quick, immediate resolution of the first phases of the painting. Don't be concerned if, in the initial colouring, it appears that all the brushstrokes stick together; if you carefully follow the suggested steps, this exercise will be easy.

The initial sketch of the landscape is very simple. The drawing, done with a brown Chinagraph pencil, involves a few curves that describe the cart tracks in the road and other voluptuous, circular shapes to locate the vegetation.

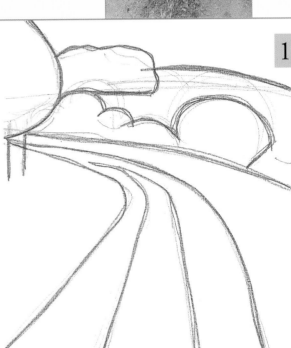

1

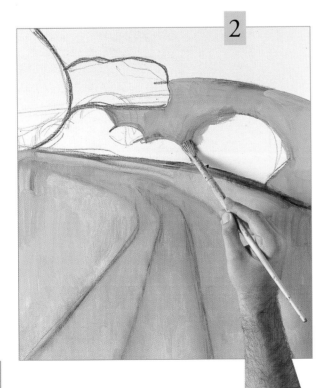

2

Tip

The technique of working in patches of colour is especially applicable with subjects that present some-what abstract shapes, such as superimposed clusters of vegetation.

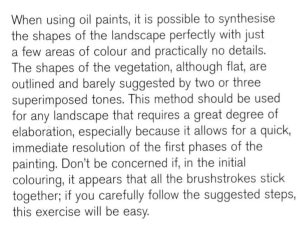

Begin by covering the ground with a raw sienna slightly diluted with turpentine, leaving the sky and the vegetation white. For painting this area of the picture, a medium brush – whether round, flat or cat's tongue – is best, although if you prefer you can use a broader one.

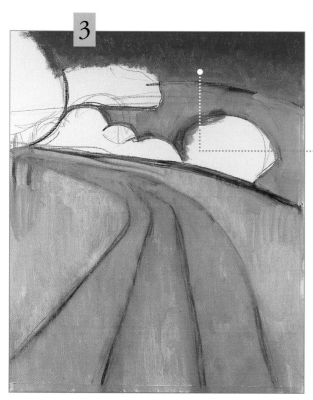

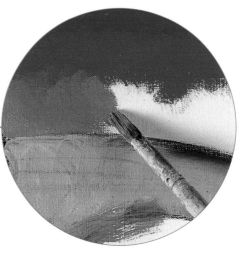

For the gradation in the sky, apply the darker colour at the top, a medium shade in the middle and the lightest blue at the edge of the hills. Once the colours are applied, you simply have to go over them repeatedly with the brush to smooth out the transitions from one shade to the next.

Paint the sky with ultramarine blue and cyan, applied to form a gradation. Many professional artists choose to lighten the shade when the sky is all one colour, a trick that gives the landscape more interest.

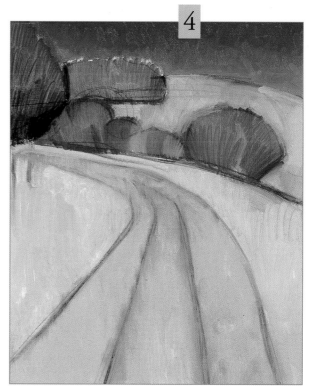

By mixing permanent cadmium green with browns, you can create different greenish shades for painting the vegetation. The colour is applied diluted with turpentine. The colour contrasts describe the structure and the shape of each cluster.

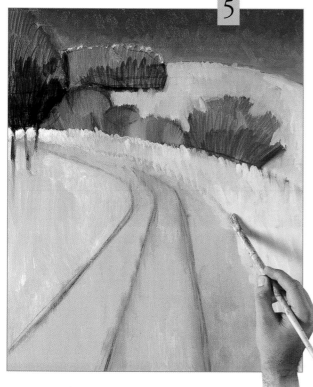

Paint the fields of dried grass on the reddish background using an ochre mixed with white. The colour is mixed with a little turpentine and applied flat on the hill in the background. In the foreground the brushstrokes are thicker; they are applied in short, vertical strokes to recreate the texture of the grass.

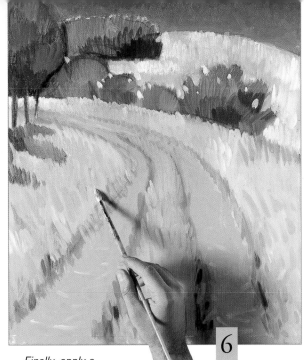

Finish up the grass in the foreground with new additions of slightly yellow ochre. The ruts of the road are left the same colour as the background to create contrast. Using burnt umber, paint the edges of the road to make it stand out more.

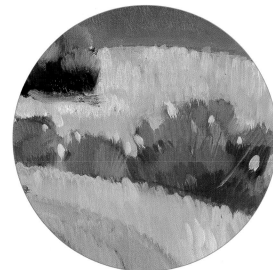

6

Finally, apply a few touches of thicker, light green paint to the crown of the pines and a violet grey to the shadows that project onto the grass. A few brushstrokes with orange ochre and yellowish ochre produce a gradation in the reddish dirt of the road. The colouring is now finished.

7

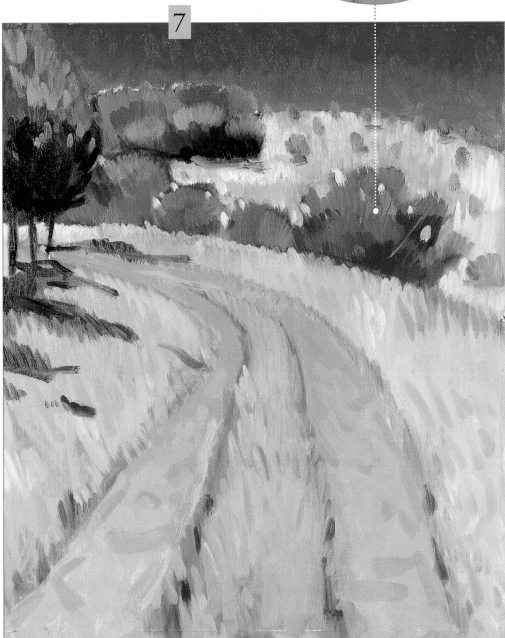

Finish the vegetation by superimposing new variations of green over the previous ones. Finish the irregular profile of the plants by adding small, light touches of paint onto the green to suggest spaces through which the background colour is visible.

Using COLOUR *for* EFFECT

Using colours to define the main chromatic areas of the landscape is one way to quickly cover the white of the canvas. As you continue to work on the painting, you can finish the coloured areas with lots of details. To better understand colour technique, let's look at several tremendously simple ways to apply colours.

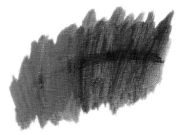

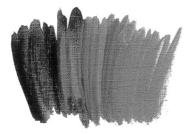

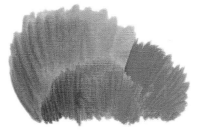

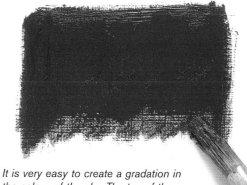

Use paint thinned with turpentine to depict vegetation. You can use different shades of green to represent the light that reaches each area.

If you wish to differentiate several planes of vegetation, give each area a different colour and present the planes as overlapping one another.

In certain areas the underlying line from the Chinagraph pencil or charcoal is visible. This is not a problem. In many cases, these lines give the work more graphic interest.

A green blotch turns into vegetation when the background is painted with thicker paint. Light ochre is used to outline the plant and apply spots onto the green to suggest spaces among the leaves.

It is very easy to create a gradation in the colour of the sky. The top of the paper is painted with a deep blue.

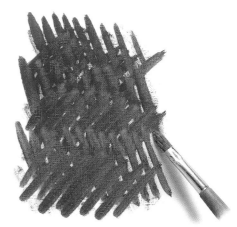

Moving down the paper two more blues are applied: a medium one and a light one.

The three strips of blue are merged by simply going over them with the tip of the brush.

These brushstrokes show the direction of brushstrokes to be used in creating gradations in the sky.

LANDSCAPE *with* VEGETATION

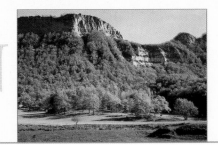

LANDSCAPE *with* *Abundant* VEGETATION

A landscape with lots of vegetation allows for a certain amount of experimentation, such as colour changes and even variations in proportions, without compromising the final result. You must select suitable colours, which do not always need to be green or brown and apply them to the canvas using brushstrokes appropriate to the shape of the trees and the texture of the foliage. The versatility of oils makes them the best medium for this exercise.

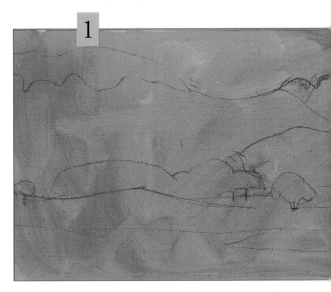

Paint an orange background using acrylic for quick drying. The first line on the canvas, done in charcoal, clearly establishes the main areas of the landscape. This involves identifying planes and outlining the shape of the mountains.

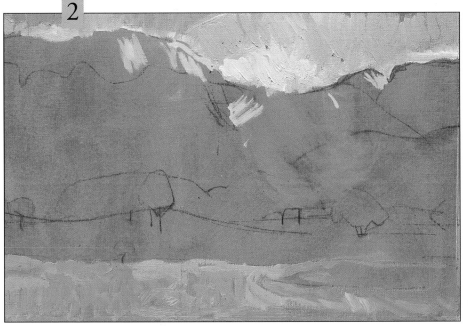

Cover the sky using thick paint in a gradation of a little ultramarine blue and lots of white. The brushstrokes should not completely cover the background, but they do define the shape of the mountains. Mix yellow, white and green and proceed in the same fashion to cover the meadow at the bottom.

Tip

The coloured background is done in acrylic; that way, it dries quickly and you can start to draw with a stick of charcoal. Working on dry paint, you can make as many corrections as you need. To erase, simply go over the area with a clean cloth.

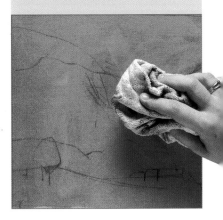

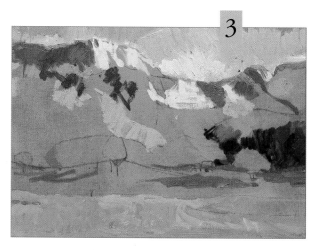

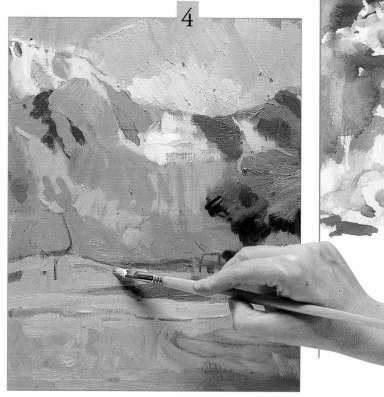

Paint the light areas and the shadows on the mountains. The shades used should be an extension of the ones in the sky: a good variety of violets and whites broken up with ochre and blue. Instead of covering up the orange background completely, leave small light areas that highlight the relief on the rocky surfaces.

Paint the vegetation using shorter, superimposed brushstrokes, and paint the meadows with additions of a flat colour that covers well. Paint the shadows cast by the trees, leaving spaces through which you can see the underlying greyish green.

Finish the colouring with slightly diluted paint. This involves covering the canvas quickly with imprecise additions of colour. The sketchy treatment of these varied green spots serves as a basis for later stages in the painting.

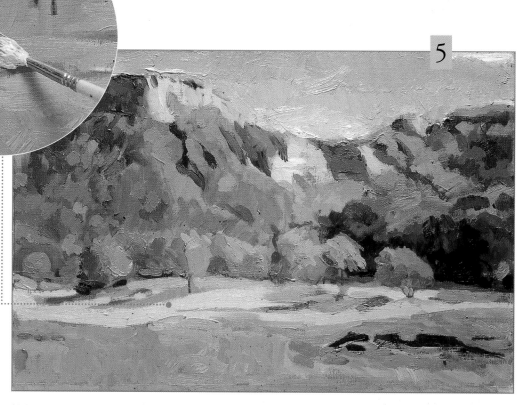

Using thicker paint, flatten the spots of colour and differentiate each plane with new additions of colour. Thus, the mountains appear ochre, yellow and violet on top; pinks are predominant in the middle zone; and in the foreground there are new variations of green.

6

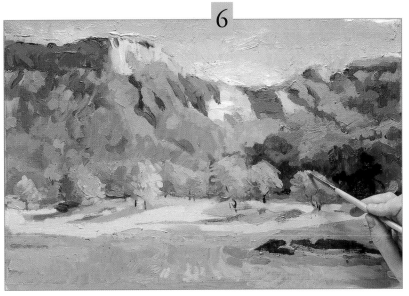

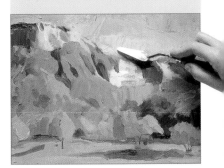

The vegetation close to the observer needs greater detail. Using a fine, round brush, superimpose strokes of paint to help communicate the texture of foliage. Notice that many of these trees are painted using juxtaposed patches of colour in the form of tonal gradations.

A painting with a great variety of colour can achieve a very finished look if you use the right colouring techniques, always working from the general to the particular. The details should not be added until the last stage: Using a fine brush loaded with colour, give greater relief to the nearby row of trees.

The trunks of the nearby trees are not done in paint, but rather by drawing onto the wet paint with a stick of charcoal.

7

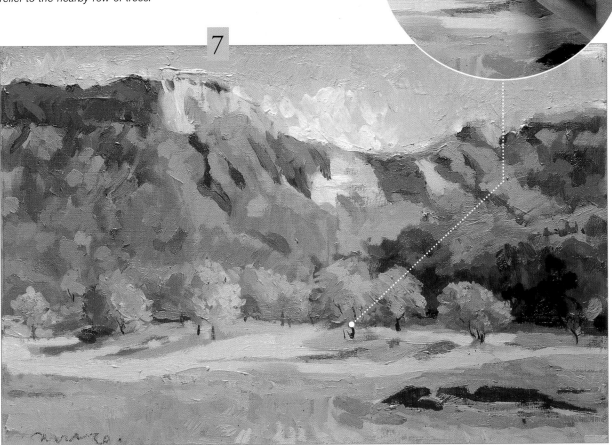

LANDSCAPE TEXTURES

Expressing the proper shape and texture of each element in the landscape makes it possible to identify the various plant species. This commonly involves a certain degree of synthesis; it is not merely a question of colour but also the manner in which it is applied. In order to describe a texture, you must use the appropriate techniques for your subject.

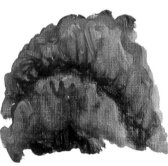

A carefully depicted tree takes on a volumetric appearance and shows a clear differentiation between light and dark areas. The successive slanting brushstrokes indicate the location of the light source.

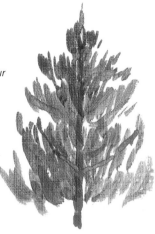

It is important to develop your ability to synthesise shapes. Carefully study the shape of every species of tree so the observer will be able to recognize them. Then use a few brushstrokes to synthesise their characteristic shape. The direction of the brushstrokes must follow the direction of leaf growth.

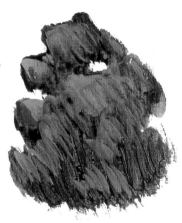

The trees in a middle plane can be represented as compact masses. The effect of volume is achieved by gradations in the green from light to dark. The texture is suggested by the brushstrokes.

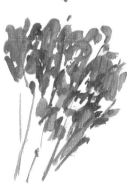

A few fine brushstrokes suffice for painting a stem and a cluster of greenish patches in a pattern to represent the foliage. It is important to leave some open spots among the leaves so that the background colour has room to breathe.

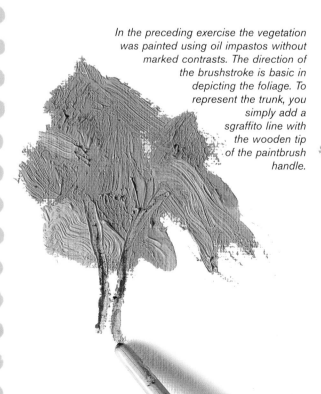

In the preceding exercise the vegetation was painted using oil impastos without marked contrasts. The direction of the brushstroke is basic in depicting the foliage. To represent the trunk, you simply add a sgraffito line with the wooden tip of the paintbrush handle.

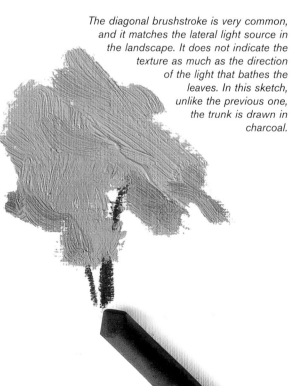

The diagonal brushstroke is very common, and it matches the lateral light source in the landscape. It does not indicate the texture as much as the direction of the light that bathes the leaves. In this sketch, unlike the previous one, the trunk is drawn in charcoal.

Superimposing PLANES

Superimposing PLANES: *Distinguishing Distances*

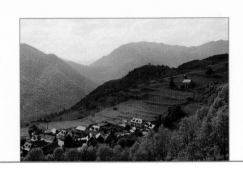

Superimposing planes and shapes, such as hills and trees, creates an illusion of depth. The eye perceives the superimposed shapes as located one behind the other, in planes that recede progressively from the observer. Shifts in light or colour can heighten the appearance of depth in the landscape. In the following exercise, you will learn how to apply this concept and control the colours in each plane. The medium used is oils.

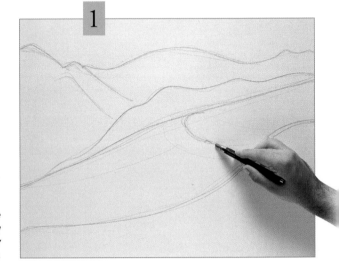

Devote more time to drawing if the model requires it. Begin by working very schematically, depicting every plane without slowing down for details.

Tip

Once the drawing is done, it is a good idea to begin painting the sky with a gradation of blue.

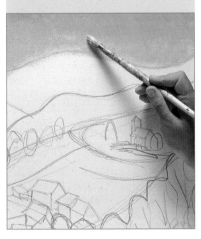

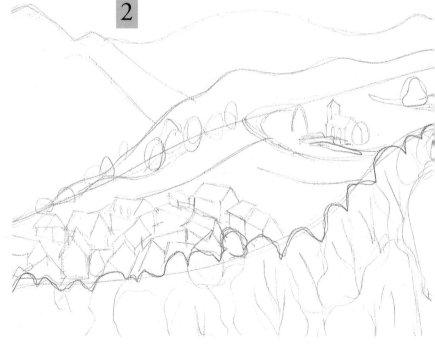

Adding to the sketch, locate the clusters of houses, the trees in the middle distance, which are represented with circular shapes and finally the approximate position of each tree in the foreground.

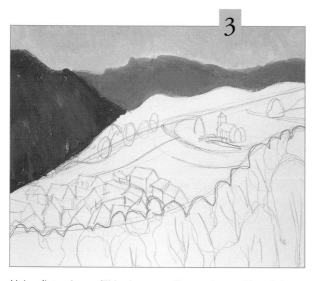

3

While the violet colour base is still wet, add relief in the mountains by applying lighter shades of violet in the illuminated areas and darker ones, some mixed with green, in the shaded areas.

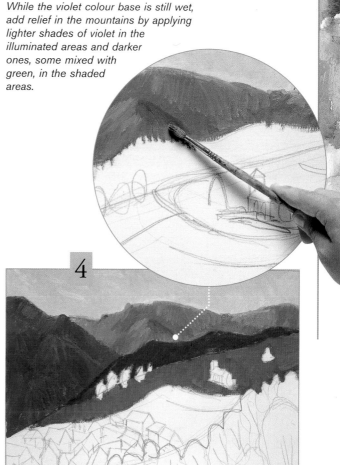

Using flat colours, fill in the most distant planes. Use violets, the shade landscapes tend to present in the distance. The further away the mountains are, the lighter the violet becomes.

4

Paint the meadows with various flat, medium greens that present little contrast but describe the terrain.

Approach the middle planes with raw sienna and green. The colours are applied opaque and flat – that is, without any gradation. Omit the trees and buildings and leave the spaces for them blank.

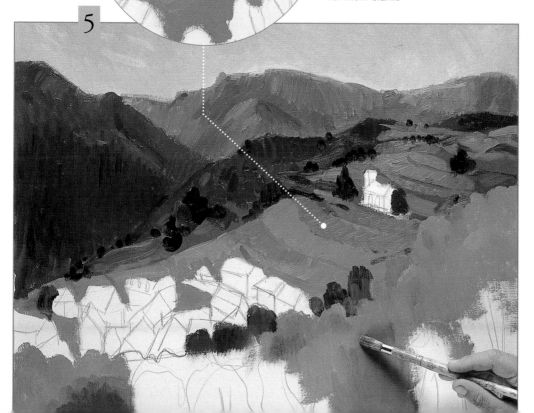

5

Finish up the fields in the middle using broad strokes of greens that are clearly differentiated. The distant trees appear in greater contrast. Paint the foliage of the cluster of trees at the bottom using spots of colour that blend together.

41

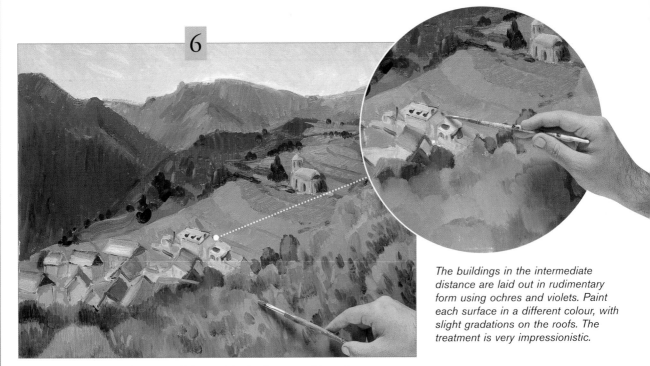

6

The buildings in the intermediate distance are laid out in rudimentary form using ochres and violets. Paint each surface in a different colour, with slight gradations on the roofs. The treatment is very impressionistic.

In order to distinguish the green of the trees in the foreground from the fields in the middle plane, we add more yellow and ochre to the foreground. The warmer the colour, the closer it appears to be.

Finish up by adding more brushstrokes in the vegetation of the foreground to create a greater effect of texture. Add short brushstrokes of ochre and yellow impasto over the initial greenish spots to create the appearance of leaves.

Tip

For a more refined treatment of the trees in the foreground, use a fine, round brush to add long, directional brushstrokes.

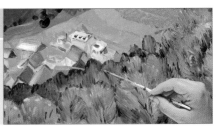

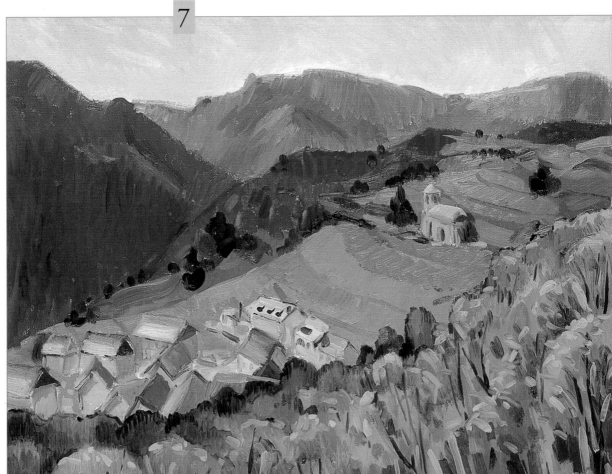

7

The DIRECTION *of the* BRUSHSTROKE

In painting a landscape it is not enough to use the proper colours; you also have to decide on the direction of the brushstrokes to depict the terrain and the texture of the surfaces most effectively. A general rule is that the brushstroke always follows the direction of the surface it describes. To better understand this concept, let's look at two landscapes painted with fine, linear brushstrokes.

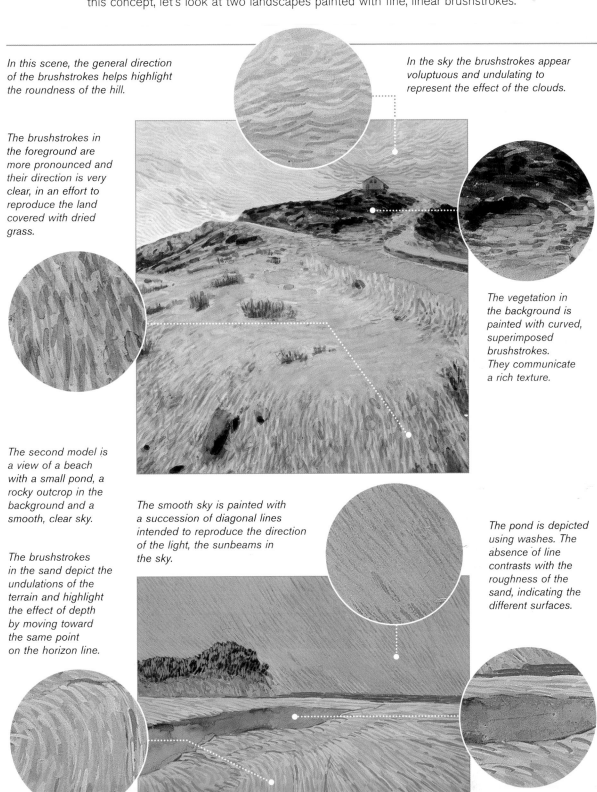

In this scene, the general direction of the brushstrokes helps highlight the roundness of the hill.

In the sky the brushstrokes appear voluptuous and undulating to represent the effect of the clouds.

The brushstrokes in the foreground are more pronounced and their direction is very clear, in an effort to reproduce the land covered with dried grass.

The vegetation in the background is painted with curved, superimposed brushstrokes. They communicate a rich texture.

The second model is a view of a beach with a small pond, a rocky outcrop in the background and a smooth, clear sky.

The brushstrokes in the sand depict the undulations of the terrain and highlight the effect of depth by moving toward the same point on the horizon line.

The smooth sky is painted with a succession of diagonal lines intended to reproduce the direction of the light, the sunbeams in the sky.

The pond is depicted using washes. The absence of line contrasts with the roughness of the sand, indicating the different surfaces.

Painting DISTANCE

Painting
DISTANCE

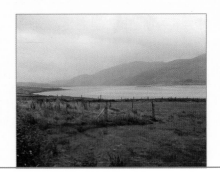

Watercolours are the ideal medium for creating subtle gradations of shade and colour using a spontaneous, direct technique. This medium is thus very appropriate for representing changing atmospheric conditions and the effect of distance in a landscape subjected to the pale light of a cloudy day. The subdued colours and soft outlines in the distant planes are produced by adding more water to the colour. Let's get some practice with watercolours.

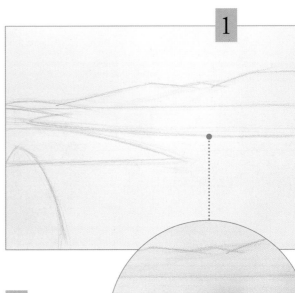

Do a simple pencil drawing. Begin by drawing the horizon line, then the shape of the mountains and finally, a few lines that locate the major features of the terrain.

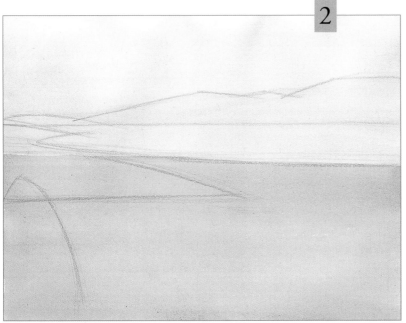

Before starting to paint, moisten the paper with clean water. The dampness of the paper allows you to spread out the colour very evenly.

The first step involves colouring in the broadest surfaces of the model with uniform colours. Cover the meadows at the bottom of the painting with a medium green on a soft brush that holds lots of water.

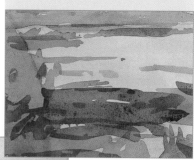

3

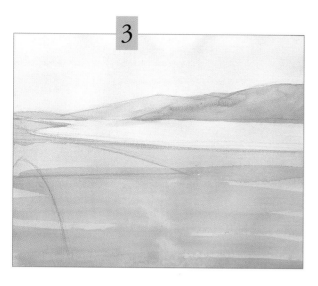

Use violet to paint the farthest plane; the mountains on the left are done in a lighter shade because they are farther away from the observer. The sky is faintly coloured in the same shades used on the mountains, but highly diluted with water.

Tip

With watercolours, painting with a reduced number of colours does not mean that the work will have a limited chromatic range. On the contrary, you can create a multitude of secondary colours and shades by superimposing glazes.

4

Add a transparent purplish wash to the sky to suggest the presence of clouds. When the green at the bottom of the painting is dry, superimpose irregular patches of ochre and brown to situate the major shapes of the vegetation.

5

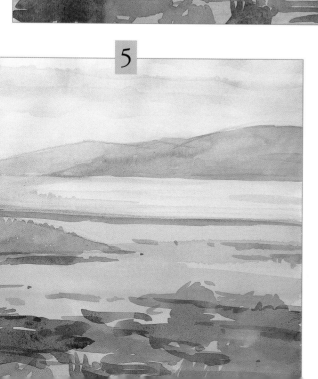

The water of the lake acts like a mirror, so it should be the same colour as the sky. To emphasize the edges of the banks, go over them with a medium hue of violet.

Before adding a new layer of colour, make sure you allow the previous washes to dry completely. To prepare the colour base in the foreground, add to the green of the land broad, horizontal brushstrokes in a slightly broken green with a bit of raw umber.

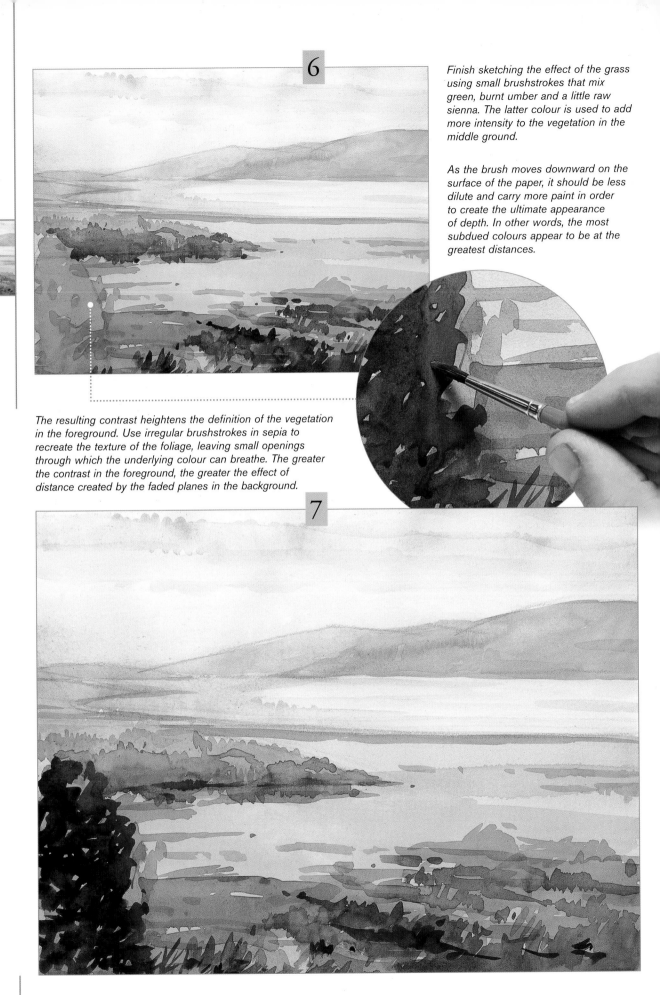

6

Finish sketching the effect of the grass using small brushstrokes that mix green, burnt umber and a little raw sienna. The latter colour is used to add more intensity to the vegetation in the middle ground.

As the brush moves downward on the surface of the paper, it should be less dilute and carry more paint in order to create the ultimate appearance of depth. In other words, the most subdued colours appear to be at the greatest distances.

The resulting contrast heightens the definition of the vegetation in the foreground. Use irregular brushstrokes in sepia to recreate the texture of the foliage, leaving small openings through which the underlying colour can breathe. The greater the contrast in the foreground, the greater the effect of distance created by the faded planes in the background.

7

USING *the* COULISSE EFFECT

The *coulisse* effect involves working with clearly differentiated bands of colour. It is, in comparison to other, more complex methods – such as painting the intervening atmosphere and projecting lines of perspective – a simple effect that allows us to give depth to a landscape. Despite its simplicity, there are several considerations that beginners should keep in mind, which are presented below.

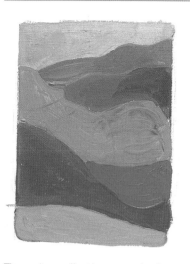

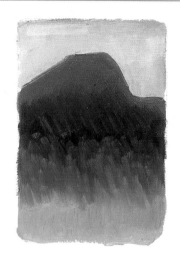

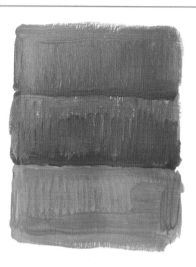

The coulisse *effect is a very simple way to suggest depth by superimposing strips of flat colour. The order of the colours is very important: Warm colour dominate in the near planes, and cold colours in the distant ones. The distribution of colours should constitute a tonal scale.*

By blending the different strips of colour to form a gradation, you can highlight the effect of depth; however, the distinction between planes seen in the previous example is replaced with a more subtle representation.

To represent different planes in a landscape, the planes must be clearly differentiated through colour changes. If you paint in a naturalist manner, these changes of shade should exhibit minimal contrast.

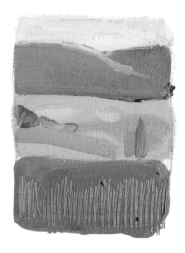

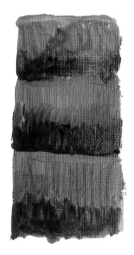

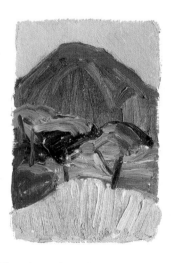

Every plane in the landscape needs a different degree of resolution. The foreground can be depicted with greater contrasts and offer textures, details and sgraffito. In the middle ground, the treatment is less detailed, and in the distance everything is reduced to broad, monochrome patches of colour.

To superimpose planes in the same colour, you can use false contrast to differentiate between them; that is, you can add a darker green as a gradation so that each band of colour can be distinguished.

When the various planes are clearly differentiated by colour, you can introduce expressive effects, such as impasto brushstrokes or striations in the foreground and background. These brushstrokes must always follow the direction of the surface represented.

47

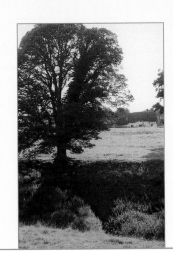

A SUNNY
Landscape

If you want a landscape to appear sunny, you must exaggerate the contrasts between the light and shaded areas; the darker the shadow appears, the brighter the direct sunlight that bathes the landscape will appear. In addition to setting up contrasts of intensity, you must also create contrasts of scale; warm colours must be present in the sunny area of the landscape and cold colours in the shadows. It is important to use pure, saturated colours, which are more expressive.

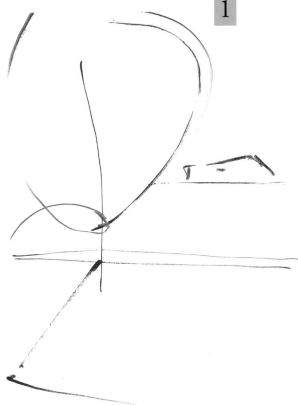

1

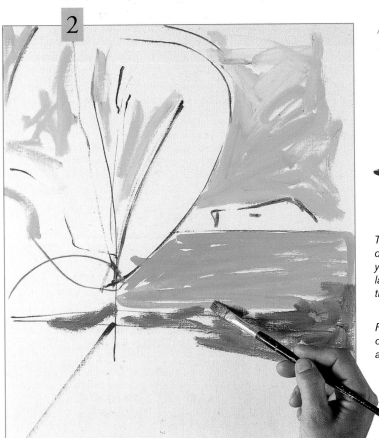

2

The sketch is done without a preliminary drawing by tracing directly on the canvas with the tip of the brush. This will help you understand the composition and the main lines of the landscape. The sketch also identifies the location of the tree, the house, and the edges of the sunny area in the foreground.

First paint the sky and the sunny field with yellow and orange, filling in the colour of the whole area, which will act as a background for the dark branches of the backlit tree.

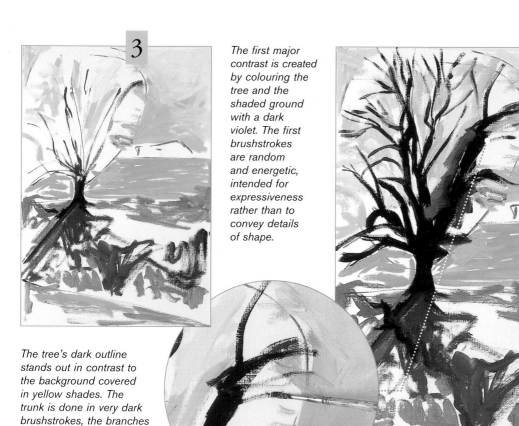

3

The first major contrast is created by colouring the tree and the shaded ground with a dark violet. The first brushstrokes are random and energetic, intended for expressiveness rather than to convey details of shape.

The tree's dark outline stands out in contrast to the background covered in yellow shades. The trunk is done in very dark brushstrokes, the branches in slightly drier lines.

4

Use a fine, rounded brush to outline the tree branches in grey, violet and black. This involves extending secondary branches from the main branches already defined.

5

Once the branches and the extensions have been painted, paint the leaves of the tree by mixing an olive green with ochre. This step is especially tricky because there is a danger of using too much impasto in the crown of the tree; it is important to paint the leaves with energy, but also with restraint.

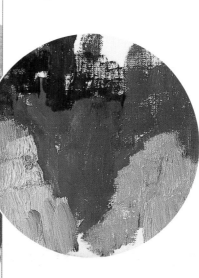

As you progress, add variations of violet to the dark ditch in the foreground. Adding shades of violet to the shadows on the ground sets up a relationship of complementary colours; that is, colours that offer the greatest possible contrast with the oranges and yellows that are present in the sunny areas.

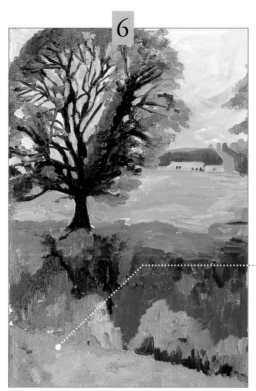

6

Using yellow mixed with a little white, carefully paint the pieces of sky that appear among the tree branches. Add new, softened greens in the middle plane. Finish the shaded area of the ditch with new brushstrokes in violet.

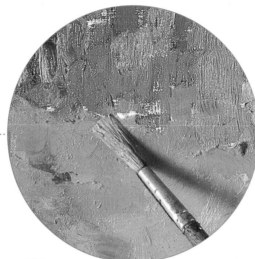

Cover the foreground with thick, dense paint. Create contrast between the sunny and shaded areas by using colours of different temperatures.

Finally, add more definition to the house in the background and some small brushstrokes in red that increase the temperature of the sunny area. A few strokes in violet contribute texture to the tree trunk.

7

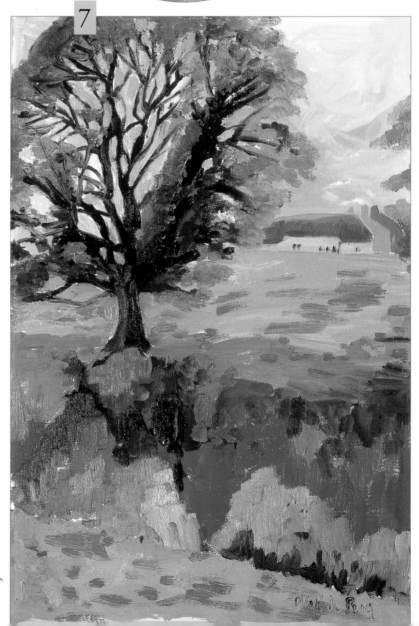

Tip

The intention of the brushstroke is very important. Consider how the colours create an impasto on the canvas as they are applied over one another.

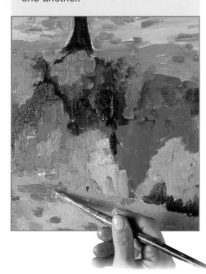

LANDSCAPE SKETCHES: A TESTING GROUND

A landscape sketch is a good way to become familiar with the various features that make up a subject. Sketching is an opportunity to note passing observations and express yourself spontaneously, using just a few brushstrokes to complete a composition in a certain range of colours or trying out a new way to apply the paint. Practising these sketches will help you develop many skills of painting: changing the viewpoint, painting at different hours of the day, trying out new materials and modifying colours.

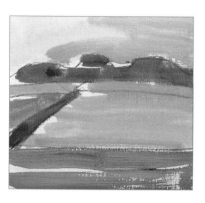

A sketch doesn't require a high degree of precision. This one was done in barely thirty seconds. A minimalist application of colour indicates the different planes that make up the landscape.

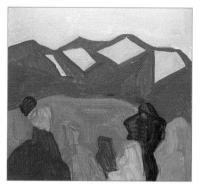

If you don't have much experience in mixing colours, you can do a sketch using flat blocks of colour in shapes of just one shade.

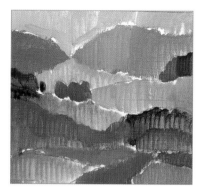

To do a good sketch, you only need to be consistent in selecting the colours and locate every plane appropriately. To achieve a feeling of spontaneity and expressiveness, you can highlight the lines and emphasize the presence of brushstrokes.

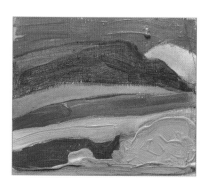

Sketching is perfect for trying out all the effects and techniques that you don't dare to apply on a larger canvas for fear of spoiling the work. It is a good way to practice with impastos and gradations.

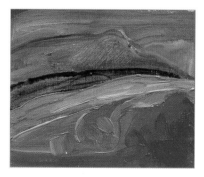

By intentionally varying the selection and arrangement of the colours, you can modify the effect of depth and the expressiveness of the sketch. Here, the river painted in yellow becomes the centre of interest in the painting; in the previous example, though, the river is scarcely noticeable and blends in with the landscape.

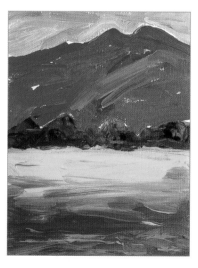

Sketches are a testing ground for trying out ways of harmonizing the features of a landscape, especially in treatments that emphasize colour.

WINTER
Landscapes

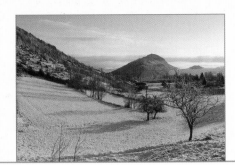

After an abundant snowfall, the colour of the grass and the vegetation is replaced by a whitish surface that acts as a light reflector. This complicates the visual interpretation of the landscape, which is flooded with cold colours. To help you learn to paint a snowy scene, this exercise shows that snow should not be painted only in white. Behind its surface beauty and brilliance are a multitude of values and tones that aid in explaining the underlying terrain more effectively. The exercise uses both acrylics and oils.

Note that acrylic plays only a minor role in this work. You will use it for prepainting in a medium violet, over which you will subsequently paint with oils.

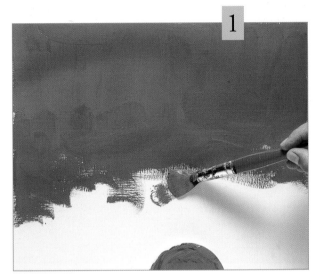

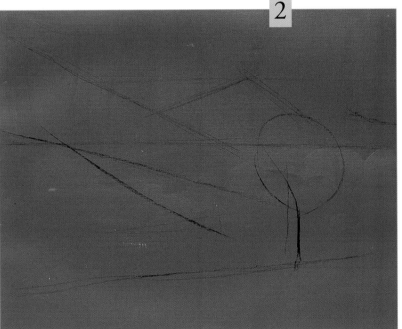

Once the layer of acrylic is completely dry, use a stick of charcoal to lay out the subject by marking a few straight lines that locate the various planes in a very general way.

Tip

The colour of the sky is very important in a snowy landscape because the light it projects directly affects the tone of the snow.

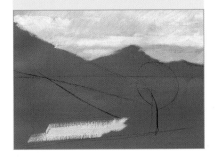

Using the same brush and a little white mixed with violet and yellow, cover the broadest areas of the landscape. Apply the colour of the snow in the form of spots using the dry brush technique, with gradations around the edges, leaving spaces for the violet in the background to breathe.

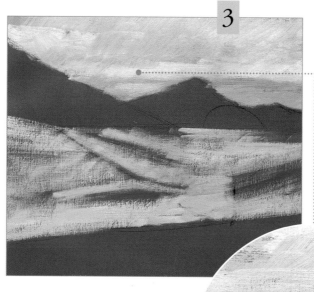

Add the trees in the background using very impressionistic brushstrokes in brown. Think of the vegetation as mere patches and avoid adding textures and details.

Apply the colour to the sky using a medium flat brush, working with thick paint only slightly diluted with turpentine.

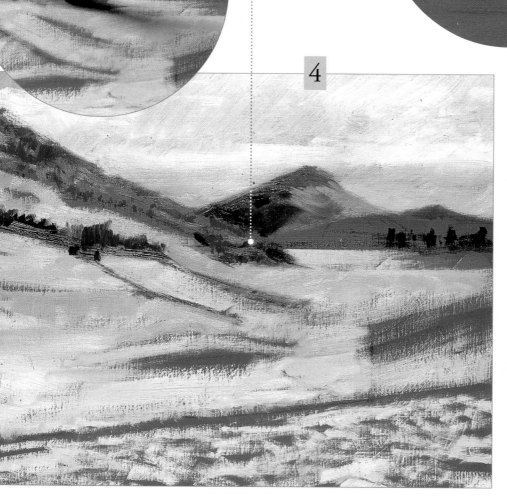

Add the snow in the foreground using well-spaced brushstrokes that reveal the violet in the background. Violet represents the shadows and helps define the irregularities in the terrain. Apply some new patches in brown in the distant planes.

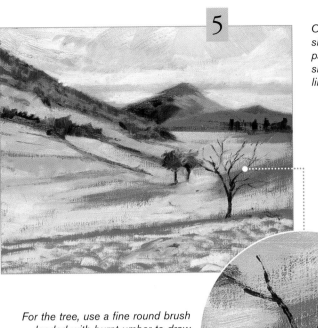

5

Create the vegetation on the mountains using different shades of brown. Moving downward through the painting, paint the two trees in the middle ground as two spots, with slight gradations that represent the crowns and darker lines for the trunks.

For the tree, use a fine round brush loaded with burnt umber to draw the vertical line of the trunk and the direction of the branches. Trees and bushes stand out in clearer profile in a snowy landscape, and they are rendered in darker colours.

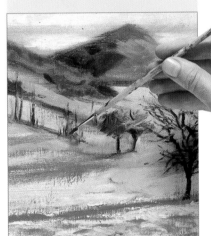

Conclude by adding brushstrokes of ochre over the previous colour to create the effect of light on the branches. Use the same brush to paint dark lines in the vegetation in the centre of the painting and new variations of white (yellowish and bluish) on the snowy ground at the bottom.

6

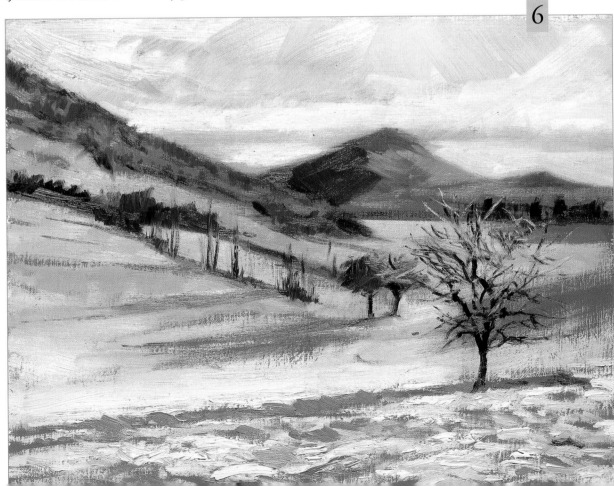

The COLOUR of SNOW

You should not think of snow as a homogeneous white mass that neutralizes the colours of the landscape, like a cloak that covers everything. In fact, a scene dominated by white can be translated into violets, ochres, blues and oranges. In the same way, it is important to make the most of brushstrokes and other effects to adequately depict the consistency and surface of snow.

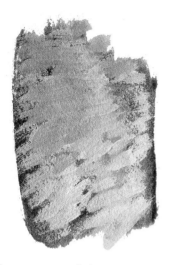

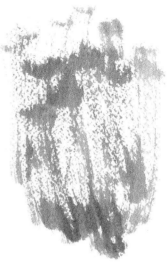

You can use small, juxtaposed brushstrokes that allow the brown of the background to show through tentatively. The brushstrokes need not be white; variations are obtained by mixing white with a little yellow or blue.

In painting snow, it is appropriate to work over a bluish, violet or brown background. Notice the texture of snow created by passing a palette knife loaded with white over the blue colour field.

When working with washes instead of impastos, it is very effective to use the dry brush technique to represent snow – that is, using a stiff brush with scarcely diluted paint that covers thinly.

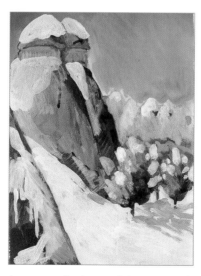

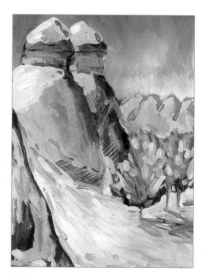

Shadows on the snow are painted in blues or violets. This sample shows snowy, undulating terrain done by blending (left) and with brushstrokes (right).

In a snowy landscape, it is not enough to cover certain parts in white. White should be used only when the sun illuminates the scene in a very direct way. You must learn to see shades of colour where there appear to be none. Compare this image to the following one.

When the sun is lower on the horizon it casts more shadows on the snow cover. Thus, the landscape offers a greater richness of tone; the whites are transformed to pinks, blues and reds.

MATTER *Painting*

LANDSCAPE *and* MATTER *Painting*

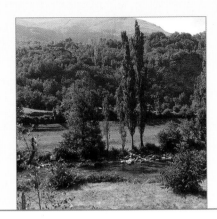

A natural landscape is one of the best subjects for matter painting, a technique that involves using dense impastos. Oils mixed with the palette knife are a very common medium.

In addition to mixing colours on the palette, palette knives are commonly used to apply the paint directly onto the canvas; they take the place of the brush and provide a new range of effects. This exercise combines these practical resources, introducing you to impastos applied with a palette knife and finished up with a brush.

Tip

Before drawing the trees, it is important to define the planes clearly. They are indicated with a series of horizontal or diagonal lines that divide the landscape into the various distances.

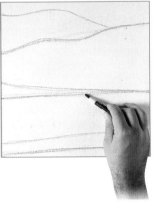

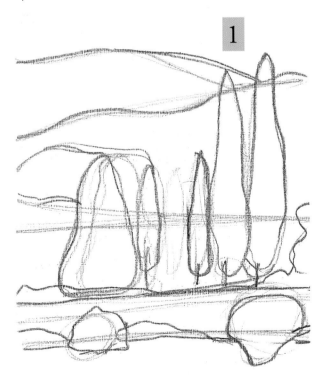

Before beginning to paint, it is advisable to sketch the main shapes. This drawing is synthetic, comprised of a few wavy lines that distinguish the planes and define the most important plant shapes.

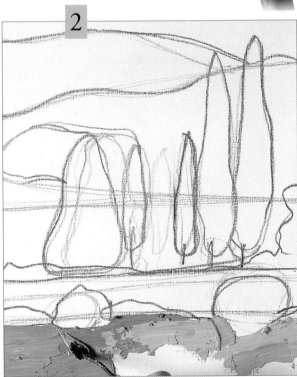

Set to work on the lower part of the picture. Cover the foreground with dense paint, a mixture of ochre, yellow, white and a touch of burnt umber. Work with the palette knife held flat to create clear differences of tone and value.

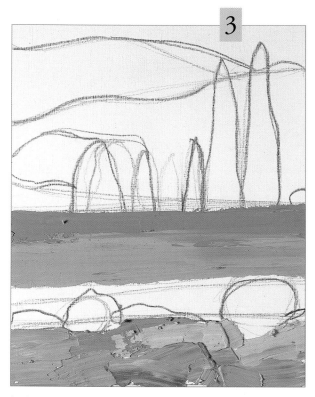

In the lower part add greenish ochre and raw sienna to give greater variety to the overall tone. Use the flat base of the blade to produce the smooth surface of the grass field in the middle ground; it is done in two tones of green that are spread out horizontally.

Tip

Applying the impastos onto the original drawing covers up the shapes and the outlines of the vegetation. You can restore them by drawing with the point of the palette knife onto the layer of fresh paint.

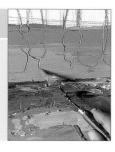

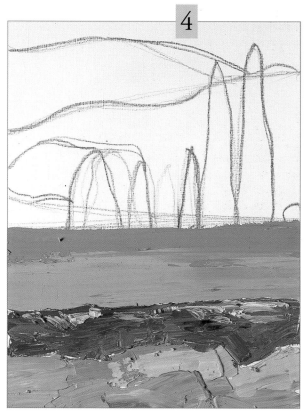

Paint the brook with the palette knife, mixing ultramarine blue and cobalt blue. The points of light on the water are pinpoint additions of white, using just the point of the palette knife to deposit the right amount of colour.

To represent the texture of the vegetation, manipulate the palette knife in an agitated, random pattern, in keeping with the irregular surface of the area being treated.

Paint the mass of vegetation in the background, enriching the greens with shades of orange and violet. The most distant mountains and the sky are also done with the palette knife, with more white added in the final mixture.

There's no reason to limit the use of the palette knife on the painting to what you can do with the blade; it can be combined with brushstrokes. Using a medium flat brush, heighten the contrast along the banks of the river by adding patches of violet and a preliminary rendition of the vegetation.

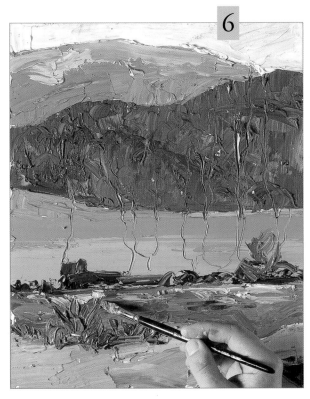

6

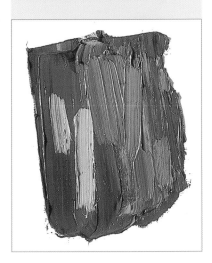

Tip

When working with paint and brush over an impasto, avoid making several passes. Otherwise the new colour will mix too much with the underlying one.

7

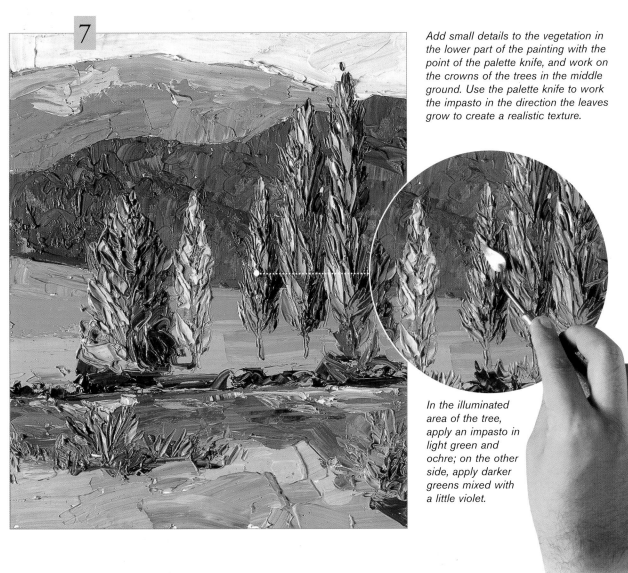

Add small details to the vegetation in the lower part of the painting with the point of the palette knife, and work on the crowns of the trees in the middle ground. Use the palette knife to work the impasto in the direction the leaves grow to create a realistic texture.

In the illuminated area of the tree, apply an impasto in light green and ochre; on the other side, apply darker greens mixed with a little violet.

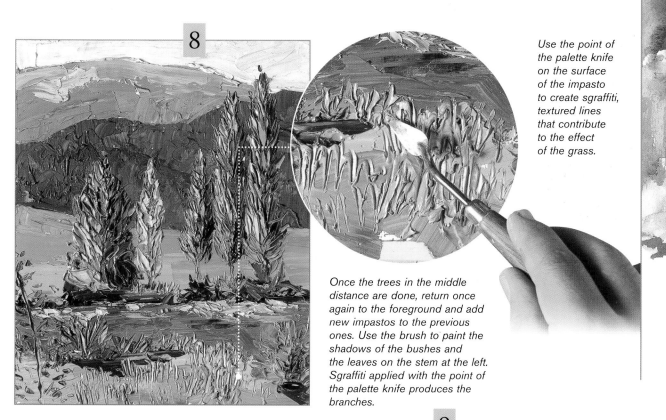

8

Use the point of the palette knife on the surface of the impasto to create sgraffiti, textured lines that contribute to the effect of the grass.

Once the trees in the middle distance are done, return once again to the foreground and add new impastos to the previous ones. Use the brush to paint the shadows of the bushes and the leaves on the stem at the left. Sgraffiti applied with the point of the palette knife produces the branches.

9

Apply the final touches with the brush. Paint a few contrasting brushstrokes on the distant mountains and thicker impastos on the surface of the water to give it more energy.

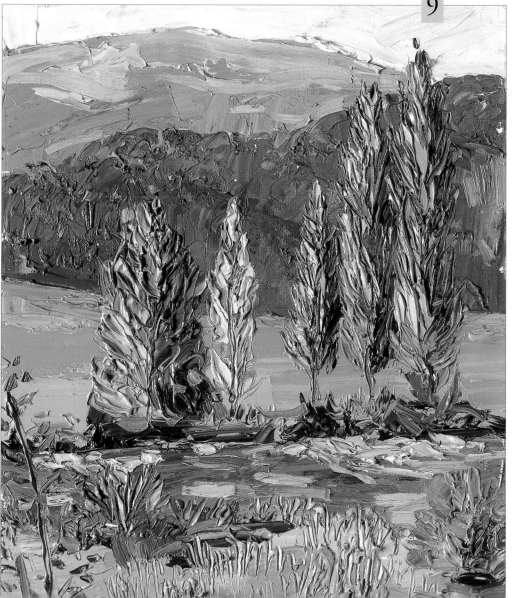

Now let's see how the preceding exercise, done by a professional artist, was completed by art students. Although the students did not paint the same model as the professional, they successfully created texture in their chosen landscapes. Their various techniques and uses of colour are worth commenting on. Learning from the work of these students should motivate you and help you progress in your work.

STUDENT
Work

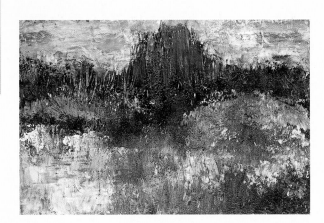

With exuberant vegetation, it is preferable to work in broad areas of colour that give the painting an abstract appearance. Differentiation among planes is achieved through strong contrasts involving bright colours. It is not necessary to paint the vegetation in green; you can use any colour on the palette. Textural effects are produced by thickening the paint with marble dust and applying brushstrokes in impasto in the upper part of the painting. Painting by Pilar Piquer.

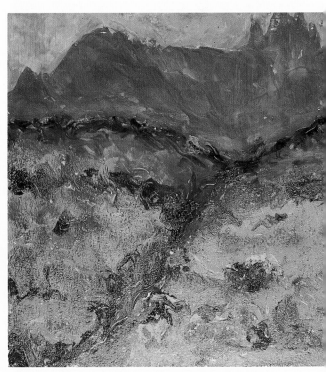

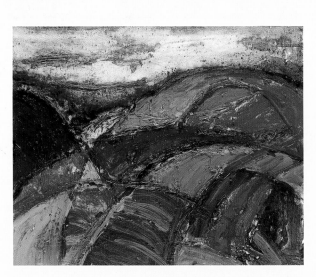

Thick, striated lines in impasto define the shape of the fields and the hills. These same textured brushstrokes break up the uniformity of the sky. An oil impasto covers every plot of land in colour and gives the painting a vigorous appearance. The colours were not mixed on the palette, but rather on the canvas, and the brushstrokes are visible. The result is a very lively painting. Painting by Gisele Messing.

When working in two clearly differentiated planes, it is appropriate to emphasize them using bold colour contrasts and different brushstrokes. Thus, the outline of the mountain farthest away from the observer is done using brushstrokes of a diluted reddish sienna and violet, creating a homogeneous surface devoid of texture. In the foreground, on the other hand, the brushstrokes take on more intensity and body, and warm colours such as red, orange and especially yellow are more prominent. Painting by Teresa Galceran.

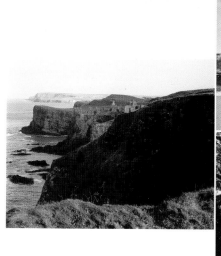
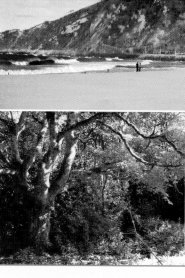
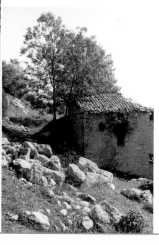

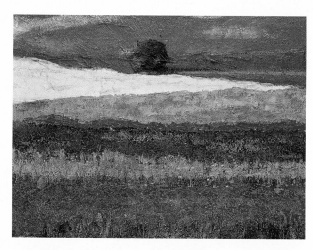

To create the granular or mottled texture of the field, the painting was first covered with a paste of gesso. Once this dries, it offers a surface that shows the brushstrokes, but it is not as abrasive as marble dust. The sections of the prepared surface are painted with bright, contrasting colours, alternating strips of warm and cold tones. Painting by Elvira Balague.

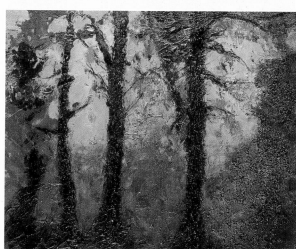

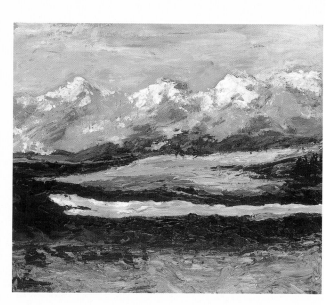

This section of woods was painted on a surface prepared with several irregular additions of marble dust. The texture makes the bark of the tree trunks more realistic, and a few brushstrokes in impasto do the same for the branches. The background of the composition is bathed in warm, light colours that make the trees stand out in greater profile through the effect of backlighting. Painting by Maria Gonzalez.

Additives such as marble dust and gesso are not always needed to create textured landscapes. Sometimes all it takes is applying lots of colour with the palette knife. The lower part of the painting was done by mixing the colour right on the canvas with small strokes that imitate the relief in the terrain. Applying paint with the palette knife permits a very effective and expressive treatment. Painting by Teresa Pijuan.

EFFECTS of LIGHT

The Forest Floor:
EFFECTS *of* LIGHT

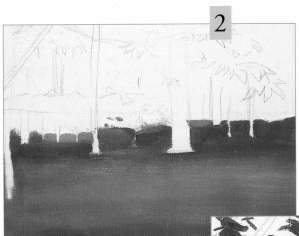

The forest floor is rich in shades, irregularities, fallen leaves and sparkles of light that penetrate the leaves of the trees. The appeal of this composition stems from the translucence of the leaves (how they are illuminated by the light that passes through them) and from the patches of light projected onto the soil. The subject was painted using acrylics.

First do a pencil sketch. There is not much spatial depth in the model, which forces you to focus on the shape of the tree trunks and their location, leaving quite a lot of space for the forest floor. There is no need to draw the leaves; you only need to suggest a few of them.

Begin by painting the broadest areas of the picture. Cover the ground with raw umber and a little ochre and white, allowing the colours to form strips with slight gradations.

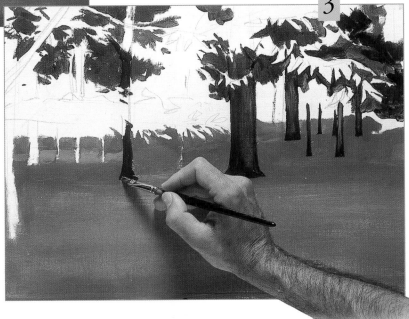

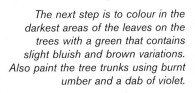

The next step is to colour in the darkest areas of the leaves on the trees with a green that contains slight bluish and brown variations. Also paint the tree trunks using burnt umber and a dab of violet.

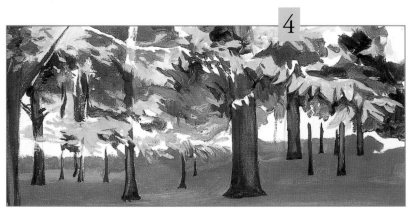

4

Over the dark patches of leaves, apply spots of a yellowish green to signify the leaves illuminated by sunlight in the foreground. Since these leaves are closer to the viewer, it is appropriate to define their shape a little more.

Finish colouring in the background spaces that are still white using bluish spots (ultramarine blue and white). Darken the background of the woods by superimposing dark brown brushstrokes on the existing reddish forest floor.

5

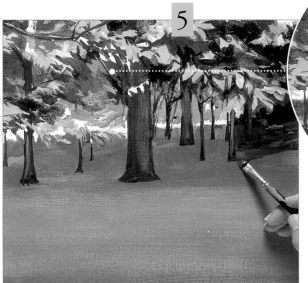

The leaves should be represented as spots that overlap one another in imprecise shapes and blend together. As a result, we never see the complete shape of a single leaf, but rather a wonderful, curious confusion. However, the direction of growth of the foliage is well defined.

The last additions of colour give the painting its overall effect. Apply a very light ochre onto the forest floor to create the effects of light on the ground. Working rapidly in a horizontal direction with a fairly dry, flat brush gives these patches an open, impressionist appearance.

6

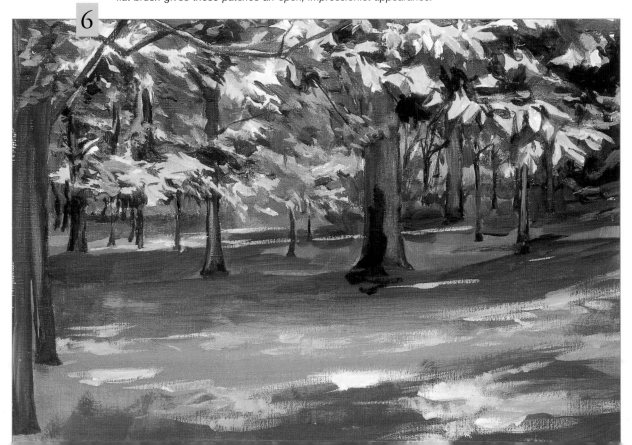

ALEXANDER COZENS
(1717–1786)

*Alexander
Cozens*

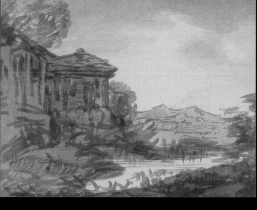

Alexander Cozens. A Villa Next to a Lake, *approx. 1770. Pencil and sepia and black inks, 6 × 7.5 inches (15 × 19 cm). Private collection (London).*

A famous British watercolourist of the eighteenth century, Cozens advocated abstraction as the basis of his compositions, using blots of colour as an organizing system for landscape and a stimulant for the imagination.

In his book *A New Method of Assisting the Invention in Drawing Original Compositions of Landscape* (London, 1785), Cozens supported the "blot" method, which involves the use of more or less accidental spots to suggest landscape: "The senses are confronted with clusters of lighter, darker and different-coloured blotches, and not with a finished shape like the ones in classical art produced through perspective, proportions and drawing."

His system was intended as a deliberate challenge to the traditional ways of painting landscape, and it arose as a new anti-academic movement to capture landscape in a more subjective way. Cozens wrote, "I regretted the lack of a sufficiently expeditious mechanical method...for extracting ideas from an ingenious mind talented in the art of drawing."

The artist advised against the traditional method of drawing in minute detail; he preferred a quick, disorderly sketch to suggest new possibilities: "There can be no doubt that too much time is wasted in copying the works of others, which tends to weaken the faculty of invention; I have no hesitation in asserting that too much time is perhaps wasted in copying landscapes from nature itself." According Cozens, there is a part of the artist's creative proce that is beyond control. He believed that perception the landscape originates in basic shapes, and his theory emphasizes randomness and the artist's capacity for synthesis: "Sketching...involves transferring ideas from the mind onto the paper...; colouring involves producing varied markings...by creating random forms..., from which ideas are presented to the mind... Sketching is delineating ideas; spots of colour suggest them."

Cozens imparted his knowledge to his followers at Eton College, instructing them to use blots to discover ways to paint landscapes. Then, a little retouching was all it took to transform those colou into a legible landscape sketch. Although blots of colour stimulate invention, they must be further refined with details to produce a painting. Cozens wrote: "The sensory datum is common to all, but th artist elaborates on it and clarifies it with his indivic mental and manual technique, and thus leads socie to a greater experience and performs an educatior purpose." It really mattered little to Cozens if the ini shape of the landscape was premeditated or improvised. What counted was what the artist chos to do with that shape.

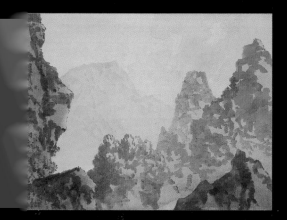

Alexander Cozens. Mountain Peaks, *1785. Sepia ink, 8.5 × 12 inches (22 × 30 cm). British Museum (London).*

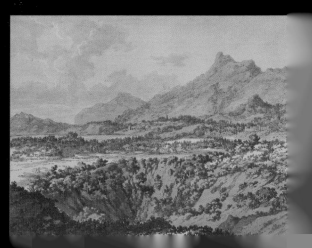

Alexander Cozens. Mountainous Landscape with a Hollow, *1785. Watercolour and ink, 9 × 12 inches (23 × 30 cm). National Gallery of Art (Washington, DC).*